SHARING A SOLDIER'S STORIES

World War II Letters from a GI

Pam Berry

ISBN: 979-8-218-90311-4

Cover and book design by Matthew McNitt.

First printing edition 2026.

To my husband, Alan Gargano,
my cousins Paul Berry and Thomas Kinney,
and my dear friends, Mark and Karen Biolchino,
who have shared this journey with me.

TABLE OF CONTENTS

Table of Contents

Preface

"Congratulations" is what most people said when I told them I was retiring at the end of the 2023, after spending sixteen years at Blue Cross Blue Shield of Michigan. But congratulations for what? For saving enough money that I'm financially able to retire? "Congratulations" seems more like something you should say when someone does a good job at something or completes a task in a timely manner — not simply stopping something.

Retirement felt more like the end of the road — the last stop before the "final" journey. I felt unhinged, unmoored; I wanted to do something meaningful with the last third of my life. In part, I suspect I missed the routine. So, I decided to tackle a project I'd been contemplating for the past dozen years or so: diving into my dad's letters from World War II and packaging them in a way that others might find entertaining, educational or inspiring.

I'd read some of my dad's letters when I was in my thirties, and found them interesting (especially references to then-current events, such as the death of Hitler or impressions of popular singers of the day, such as Frank Sinatra) but I didn't have time to concentrate on their contents. In truth, I didn't really want to finish them, as having some still-unread letters was a way of keeping him alive: I was able to keep looking forward to new conversations. Once I perused them all, I felt ready to share excerpts with others. Since my dad was such a prolific letter writer, I knew I couldn't include the entire body of letters; people's attention spans simply aren't long enough, especially these days when people are used to reading short "sound bites."

While I knew family members would be interested in my dad's story, I had to consider: Why would anyone else care? My answer to that question is that my dad had an outlook on life that served him

My dad and I in 2002, about three months before he passed away.

well, both in the business world and among family and friends —
one that might work effectively for others, as well.

He truly loved everyone, with only one or two exceptions over
the course of this life, and they, in turn, typically loved him back.
He had a positive outlook, and his outlook — essentially his
philosophy of life — tended to create positive outcomes. It was a
philosophy that Norman Vincent Peale later popularized in his
book, The Power of Positive Thinking, in the 1950s.

I've grouped excerpts from his letters into various categories,
organized by chapter, so the reader can refer to areas of special
interest, such as Army Life, Recreation and Leisure, Contemporary
References, and so on. Each chapter's contents are presented in
chronological order, beginning with his military training across
various sites in the United States.

Where possible, I've included the actual dates of the letters where
the excerpts appear. In other instances, I've made an educated
guess as some first pages of letters were missing.

Revisiting this span of my dad's life made me reflect on my own.
When I was close to completing the book, I had an epiphany:
the end of things is merely the transition into something new,
something fresh, something to welcome. I began to realize that
retirement wasn't really the end at all, but rather an opportunity
to start something new. Retirement gave me freedom to tackle a
project that was personally meaningful to me. It also gave me the
opportunity to potentially affect people's lives, something I felt
able to do while working in Communications at Blue Cross —
something I had really missed.

Pam Berry

Chapter 1
The War Years: A Brief Overview

My dad once told me he didn't realize his first name was Thomas until he entered the Army at the age of nineteen. His family and friends referred to him as Don or Donald, which was his middle name, to differentiate him from his mother's brother Tom, whom he was named after. Whether he learned of his "real" first name because his mother shared his birth certificate with him prior to enlisting or whether the Army determined his full name through resources of its own is something of a mystery as I never asked for details.

My dad had several formal photos taken of himself during his Army career. This one seemed best to capture his "joie de vivre."

In any event, he was born Thomas Donald Berry on January 6, 1924 in the city of Loretteville, Quebec, now part of the expanded city of Quebec. The family moved to Detroit in 1926.

In his later years, he often fantasized about writing his life story. In fact, when he experienced a period of cardiac psychosis, a mental health condition, after open heart surgery in his seventies, he would get up in the middle of the night and begin dictating his story into a tape recorder. While the condition, often characterized by confusion and disorientation, was thankfully short-lived, I also knew he felt he had a story to tell.

My dad in front of his house on Russell Street in Detroit. An inscription on the back, probably written by his sister, Dorothy, reads: "Gee, that's a cute one."

My dad entered the U.S. Army toward the start of World War II on March 19, 1942 — about eighty-one years to the date I began writing these words. The U.S. declared war on Japan after the bombing of Pearl Harbor on December 8, 1941. Three days later, Germany declared war on our country — and we followed it up the same day with a declaration of our own — so we were fighting in two theaters. My dad was part of the European theater and served in Fourteenth Field Artillery Observation Battalion, called the Fighting 14th.

I'm guessing he enlisted rather than being drafted since he wasn't a U.S. citizen at the time. He became an American citizen after receiving his Certificate of Naturalization in late March of 1944 — something he boasted about in a letter home two days later: "Well, Dad, as of Monday, I am now a full-fledged citizen. That's right. A real American citizen. I finally took my oath and received the papers and now feel pretty good about the whole deal."

A somewhat faded photo of his battalion. He is third row from bottom at far right, standing off to the side a bit. On the back of the photo, he has had each of the guys pictured write their names and addresses.

His first couple years in the Army were spent crossing the country by train to various training facilities, including Fort Custer, Michigan; Fort Sill, Oklahoma; Camp Roberts, California; and Fort Lewis, Washington. Why such a long period of training? In one of his letters, he suggests that the reason was that they weren't quite sure what to do with his battalion.

In July of 1944, they'd figured it out. His boots hit the ground in France in August, four months prior to the Battle of the Bulge, which he fought in. This punishing German offensive, launched in the Ardennes region of Belgium and Luxembourg, lasted approximately forty-one days. American casualties were around 80,000 to 89,500 (including approximately 19,000 killed). Despite such enormous casualties, the Allied Forces emerged victorious when the battle ended on January 25, 1945. It was the last major German offensive campaign on the Western Front, and a significant turning point in the war.

Overall, my dad seems to have adjusted to Army life pretty quickly. In a letter to his family, dated April 18, 1943, he writes:

"I am getting pretty used to being away from home by now. At first, I missed you all quite a bit, especially when we had some guys who were always complaining about the Army, but now I'm with some of the guys that are really swell. For the most part, they have been here longer than me, and they are a big help. They are always helping me on things that are tough for me and always giving me tips on this Army life that really help. And things like that really make it easier, and make you feel good. When anyone in our barracks gets any cookies or candy from home, we all eat it. It lasts for about five minutes."

A month later, in a letter that seems to illustrate how views of the government and the military have changed over the years, he writes that he and his fellow soldiers spent an hour and a half at a movie explaining why we were fighting the war. He comments that the movie was really good. It was obvious that he was gung ho about the war's mission and efforts to promote the cause, as were the vast majority of Americans at that time.

One of the more interesting aspects of the letters is his references to contemporary life. He talks about current events, movies, songs and entertainers, ranging from radio shows featuring Bob Hope and Red Skelton ["Those guys are nuts!" he writes in a letter from 1943], to hearing the news flash that Hitler died. Sometimes, he uses language that would be considered politically incorrect today, such as "Boy, I hate Hitler and his little Jap friend."

He also uses plenty of slang that was popular in the 40s. For example, in a letter dated June 20, 1943, he writes that the radio was playing "Deep Purple." His review? "Solid." Another favorite word: "swell."

Many of his comments suggest his naivete, having attended Catholic schools throughout his youth. After listening to Your Hit Parade, a popular radio show of the time, he writes to his girlfriend (later my mom), "Helen, can you tell me something? Last Saturday night I was listening to Hit Parade. Frank Sinatra was singing and those women were actually moaning. Why?" Apparently, the reactions to Sinatra foreshadowed what we later saw with Elvis and the Beatles.

Following the Allied invasion of Normandy in June of 1944, my dad's battalion came under the command of General George S. Patton, "Old Blood and Guts." He was proud to say he was part of Patton's Third Army, and thoroughly enjoyed the 1970 film Patton, which he took me and my mom to see.

In July of 1944, he shipped out to England, later continuing through France, Luxembourg, Belgium, Holland and Germany, before beginning the long journey home in September of 1945. Along the way, he picked up a Bronze Star Medal during the Battle of the Bulge, received for changing an ambulance tire under enemy fire. The medal is a military decoration for heroic or meritorious achievement or service in a combat zone.

Unfortunately, none of his letters contain any details about battles. Service members were under strict orders not to write home about their military activities. As the slogan of the day went, "Loose lips sink ships."

In his letters from France, for example, he writes things like, "Here are the names of four towns in France we visited," as he had been told not to divulge more than the names of four towns per letter. He must have done a pretty good job of adhering to instructions as I only recall one letter where a word was removed by the censors.

As a result of these restrictions, his letters home often read more like a travelogue than a description of war. In many ways, he had a good time during his war years, despite the rigors of basic training, drills and other hardships of Army life. In fact, in conversations after the war, he often referred to his experience overseas as his "European vacation paid for by the U.S. government." When I mention this to friends or acquaintances whose dads were also in the war, they often look horrified by that comment. Apparently, their dads had much tougher experiences than my dad did, or perhaps he was just more resilient or happy-go-lucky.

It seems my dad's experiences in the Army colored the rest of his life and how he interacted with people. Upon reading an early draft of my book, a former colleague at Blue Cross commented that my dad's story brought to mind author Joseph Campbell's concept of the "monomyth," commonly referred to as "the hero's journey," which he developed in The Hero with a Thousand Faces — a book I had also had read many years ago. In simplest terms, with the monomyth, a heroic protagonist sets out, has transformative adventures, and later returns home. The object, blessing or knowledge acquired during the adventure is then put to use in the everyday world.

I found it interesting to contemplate how my dad's philosophy of life, further honed during his years of military service, was later reflected in the way he lived his life after the war. As I wrote in the Preface, his philosophy seemed to mirror that of Norman Vincent Peale, author of The Power of Positive Thinking, that a positive outlook results in positive outcomes — that what you put forth in life often comes back to you.

I am struck by how his belief in — and love for — his fellow human beings helped to shape his successes in the Army, as well as in the business world in later years. His rapport with other enlisted men and commanding officers had a great deal to do with how he was able to thrive and even enjoy his war years at times.

Cast of Characters

The following chapters include excerpts from letters to his girlfriend (later his wife and my mom), Helen Smith, whom he sometimes called "Smitty," and to his family back home. His family included: his mom, Sadie (sometimes called "moms"); his dad, Walt; his brother, Earl (sometimes spelled "Earle"); his brother, Wally (sometimes referred to as "Junior"), his brother, Kenny (16 years younger than my dad) and his sister Dorothy (sometimes called Dot).

My dad with his girlfriend, Helen Smith (later his wife and my mom), at left, and his sister, Dorothy.

Chapter 2
Army Life: The Not-So-Gory Details

My dad never wrote much about his combat experience — probably due to concerns about the censors or admonitions not to worry the folks at home — but he wrote frequently of Army life in general, particularly the comradery he experienced with his fellow soldiers. For more of the nitty-gritty details of Army life, readers may want to check out the writings of Ernie Pyle, the Pulitzer Prize-winning war correspondent who was killed by enemy fire in 1945.

This postcard was sent to his brothers in March of 1943, shortly after he enlisted. It reads, in part, "I am sitting in a barber chair about to get my hair cut."

April 18, 1943: I am getting pretty used to being away from home by now. At first, I missed you all quite a bit, especially when we had some guys who were always complaining about the Army, but now I'm with some of the guys that are really swell. For the most part, they have been here longer than me, and they are a big help. They are always helping me on things that are tough for me and always giving me tips on this Army life that really help. And things like that really make it easier, and make you feel good. When anyone in our barracks gets any cookies or candy from home, we all eat it. It lasts for about five minutes.

April 22, 1943: This morning we got up as usual at 6:30, ate breakfast and made our beds. At 7:30 we were all called out for police duty. That is, we all helped clean up a section of the grounds.

April 27, 1943: Our living quarters are clean. They are washed twice a week. Clean bedding once a week. And [the floors] are always kept swept. So you couldn't ask for much more. Also, amusement is plentiful. Dances, shows, the PX, recreation rooms and Lawton City [Oklahoma], which is only four miles from here.

April 29, 1943: Today I had latrine orderly [duty] and really had a soft job. All I did was to sit around all day long. And did I love that. Starting tomorrow we get up at six instead of six-thirty. That's so we may have more exercise.

We had "Parade Retreat" tonight. There are six batteries, which compose a battalion. In this, there are approximately 1,200 men. We all marched nine abreast on the parade grounds and to you it would seem impossible for all those men to keep in the same step. But they do, by the help of a Negro band. Honestly, it's really beautiful.

- May 11, 1943, Fort Sill Oklahoma

April 30, 1943: Remember when you asked me if I liked the Army, its food and if they treated me right and I answered yes. Well, the funny part is that I couldn't very well say no. There was a captain and two lieutenants besides a sergeant and a corporal when I made the call. They just grinned when I answered your questions. But this is OK.

Today I got my Army driver's license, and it makes me feel pretty good. There were only about eight fellows who got them out of 74. This license allows me to drive all Army vehicles from a quarter ton — that is the jeep — up to the four ton, which is a six-by-six (six-wheel drive) with eight to 10 tires on it. They sure are big babies but they handle pretty nice and boy, what brakes (air brakes) on them. I think that I will get plenty of chance to drive.

My dad labeled this photo "My truck." One of his duties was to drive the officers wherever they needed to go.

May 13, 1943:   Yesterday we were kept pretty busy, I spent most of the time driving one of those big trucks (six-by-six to 10 wheels). Did I have a good time driving through the fields. But the bad part of it was that we had to run the obstacle course with a full field pack and rifle. Close to 60 pounds. It really was tough, but it wasn't too bad. I guess I am starting to get in condition after all.

Tomorrow morning, I have to get up at 5 a.m. You guessed it right the first time: I have the honored position of KP again. It will last until about nine at night. Think of the overtime and a half. I'm not getting it for doing anything wrong, but because it is my turn.

May 16, 1943: You know, Helen, this Army life isn't so bad. For instance, some sergeant will walk up to a group of fellows and ask for a volunteer. He usually asks for three guys: "You, you and you can come along." You can't win.

May 21, 1943: This morning we spent an hour and a half at a movie. It showed why we are fighting this war. It showed before we entered this war: Hitler making all his promises about not wanting war. Then it shows how he cracked down on Holland, Denmark, Belgium, Luxembourg and France. Also, the evacuation of Dunkirk. Really good.

June 2, 1943: Right now, I am sitting on my bunk in front of the door, with a nice breeze coming through. Not much new has happened since my last letter except I am more tired than ever, if that's possible. Today we had to run the obstacle course with a full [60 pound] pack and gas mask. Really misery at its ninth degree. Tonight I feel pretty good, even if I did get bawled out for not polishing my shoes at retreat. In fact, I like Army life swell today. Most likely by tomorrow I'll feel like walking home, and trying to get a date with a "certain you-know-who."

June 8, 1943: Believe it or not I just got off guard duty, and I started yesterday evening at 6. Boy, it was tough even if I did drive a Jeep all the time. Boy, Earle, they are more fun to drive than anything you have ever driven. You can get 25 out of them in first like a flash. What pickup. The speed limit up here is 20 and 25 but they handle nice around 45.

June 20, 1943: Last Friday we got back to the barracks after a strenuous week in the field… All we did was dig foxholes, work, walk and dodge snakes, tarantulas, spiders, ticks, chiggers and what else have you.

> *If you don't care for snakes, particularly rattlers, don't visit Oklahoma. While out there we killed approximately 30 of the rattler type. I myself killed one and also knocked one out of my bed. That was the night I didn't sleep very good.*
>
> *- June 20, 1943, Fort Sill, Oklahoma*

July 16, 1943: This morning we had a nine-mile hike and did it in two hours. Boy, we really had to go — on the average of four-and-a-half miles an hour. Then this afternoon we had practice in convoy with two-and-a-half ton trucks. I drove for three-and-a-half hours. My back is practically killing me from driving over field, ditches, etc. Now they have me teaching some of the fellows how to drive. Confidentially I don't believe I know much more than they do…

The sergeant in my tent said I was to drive a jeep on maneuvers. If they are held in Oregon, and we drive, I am supposed to have as passengers a colonel and first lieutenant of Survey. In a way, I hope we drive because it is better than 900 miles and I will see lots of new country.

August 18, 1943: Today we received word that we are to leave here Saturday. Destination is Oregon. And that will be our home for the next two months at least, and it sure won't be any picnic. This morning, we were issued another blanket, which makes a total of three, and also our mosquito netting. The way it looks now we are going to have some rough weather up there.

September 7, 1943: Tonight finds me sitting beside the campfire. Seeing as all the fellows have turned in by now, it is pretty quiet. The only company I have are a few lonely coyotes howling their lungs out. But they aren't alone. We are in the same boat.

It is really a beautiful night out. The sky is clear with a bright moon peeping over the trees, and the sky studded with stars… Nights like these are what make you think of home, and one sort of thinks of what he would be doing now if he was at home. I guess I do get a little homesick as much as I dread it. But I just have to puff a little harder on my pipe when that starts. Lately, it's been burning out pretty fast…

Yesterday we were in the field from eight in the morning til 7:30 at night. Today we didn't do much but get our equipment straightened out and cleaned. This afternoon we were taken in to town for a hot shower. Really nice for a change. Then tonight I had guard duty from seven until eleven. Believe me, this Army will either make me or break me. Already I can hear the bones snapping.

September 11, 1943: Today I was kept quite busy but it was for my own benefit. I had a lot of washing to do and I really made a job of it. The only thing wrong about it was that I made a great mistake. I tried to wash four pairs of dirty socks with my underwear and towels. Seems as if I now have signs of tattletale grey. By the way, Smitty, we now have a new member in our exclusive club. He's a small four-legged creature. So I have named him J.B.

after one of our sergeants. The reason is the sergeant is always eating and so is the dog.

My dad with one of his Army buddies and one of the many dog friends he picked up along the way. He writes to my mom: "I have named him J.B. after one of our sergeants. The reason is the sergeant is always eating and so is the dog."

Today I was on my way to the showers. I noticed that J.B. could stand one so I took him along. After lathering him up good, I figured he was pretty clean. So I started to dry him with my towel, but I guess we all make mistakes. Anyway, I have one more towel to wash now.

I've also undertaken the job to teach him to ride on the hood of my weapons carrier. So far I haven't had much success. Seems as if he can't stay on top. I believe the law of gravity has something to do with it. At present he is lying at my feet trying to get some rest.

September 24, 1943: Around eight-thirty last night, I received your letter. And to be absolutely truthful I figured that something must have happened because it was the first letter in six days from you.

No sooner had I finished reading it when the first sergeant tells me that I am to help deliver a crop of new trucks about a hundred miles from our camp. Well, I helped and then brought a truck back full of fellows. We got back around four in the morning, just in time to help break camp. The result was since Wednesday evening I have had exactly two hours of sleep. I am practically dead.

October 2, 1943: The day before yesterday it started, and I have been busy ever since. Sunday we arrived at our bivouac area, lined our trucks up and pitched our tents. The first thing I did was to fuel up my truck. After that, I started my washing. Honest, you would be surprised at the amount of dirty clothes that can pile up. After that was finished, I spent the rest of the time cleaning up my rifle and the rest of my equipment.

Yesterday I was kept busy all morning and most of the afternoon getting my truck ready for inspection. It had to be gassed, oil changed, battery checked, greased and the motor dusted off. Which is quite a job out here in this dust bowl.

October 8, 1943: For the last three days we were supposed to be in rest camp, but we didn't get much time to rest. The first day we spent all our time on cleaning our trucks and rifles, the next two we spent out in the field.

On our last "problem," we really had a miserable time. All we did was work from early morning until late at night. Sometimes we didn't finish until eleven or twelve. Besides that, we worked in dust all the time. But that's all in the past. It's the present that counts.

During the course of this problem, we are to work in the vicinity of Fremont National Forest. And it's really nice. And today we are surveying along the main highway. The nice part of that is we can see all the civilian cars go by. But it also makes one think of better times.

For a change, we have a nice place to stay. All around us are large
pine and redwood trees. Some of them are so tall that one feels like
an ant besides them.

November 21, 1943: All the way from Chicago [after a
furlough] I had a swell seat. It was one of those type that fold back.
That way, I could rest better. The only bad part of it was that I was
headed back to the old GI life. But now that I am here, it isn't so bad.

In Chicago, I met five of the fellows, and that made it pretty nice.
That way I didn't feel so darn lonesome. Anyway, I wasn't the only
fellow that bad — the whole damn train was more like a funeral
home than a public conveyance. When we arrived in Tacoma at
eleven this morning, I met around eight other of the fellows. We all
were sure glad to see each other. It seemed like a family reunion.

A snapshot of the barracks at Fort Lewis.

December 16, 1943: We were supposed to be out in the field for nine days, only they extended it to thirteen. And it was hell… You know, I don't believe I ever spend a worse two weeks than the last ones. It was even worse than the whole three months of the Oregon maneuvers. The hard part was we hardly ever had a decent meal, and the other was we were not allowed fires. It was just cold and damp. Especially in the forest.

February 4, 1944: Tuesday I pulled a heck of a job. I had to drive some officers around in the morning. But in the afternoon, I just kept the command car, and picked up a buddy of mine and went for a ride, which lasted about three and a half hours. That part was fun.

Now I have the distinction of being the first man in our battery to talk himself out of a guard [duty]. The fellows want my technique. Don't ask me how I did it, all I know is that I blew my top. And it worked for a change.

- February 22, 1944, Fort Lewis, Washington

Wednesday we just went out in the field and did some surveying. And it was miserable, all rain and mud. Last night, we finally had to go over the infiltration course again, and it was really rough. If I ever complain about dirty work at home again, I deserve to be clubbed.

February 20, 1944: I am in my last day of bubble dancing (K.P.) and I can't say as I am sorry. Because a week of that work gets plenty monotonous.

February 22, 1944: Junior probably told you that Thursday and Friday I was busy out on the firing range, firing the rifle and carbine. That's one thing I don't get tired of. It's a lot of fun… After firing all day Friday, I came back to camp to find myself on detail to drive a GMC 2-1/2-ton truck. They wanted me to drive a bunch of fellows that were shipping across to the

My dad relaxing in his barracks at Fort Lewis, Washington. He labels it, "Taking it easy in one of my off moments." The photo display includes a couple of glamour shots of my mom.

One of several glamour shots of my mom that she sent to my dad.

depot. I didn't get off til 9:30 that evening. That itself wasn't too bad, but after I finished driving, I noticed my name on the list for patrol guard for Saturday night. After seeing that, I was what is commonly known as pissed off. So right off I hunted up the first sergeant and argued my way out of guard duty.

March 19, 1944: It was just one year ago today that I pulled up stakes, and started out [to work] for my Uncle Sam… One year is a long time to be gone from home. But to be truthful, I can't say that the time seems long or short. Mostly it depends on the mood I'm in… Any way one looks at life in the Army, it isn't like home sweet home, and it never will [be].

Well, mom, I don't know how to start the rest of this letter, but I guess you have been sort of expecting it… You might as well know

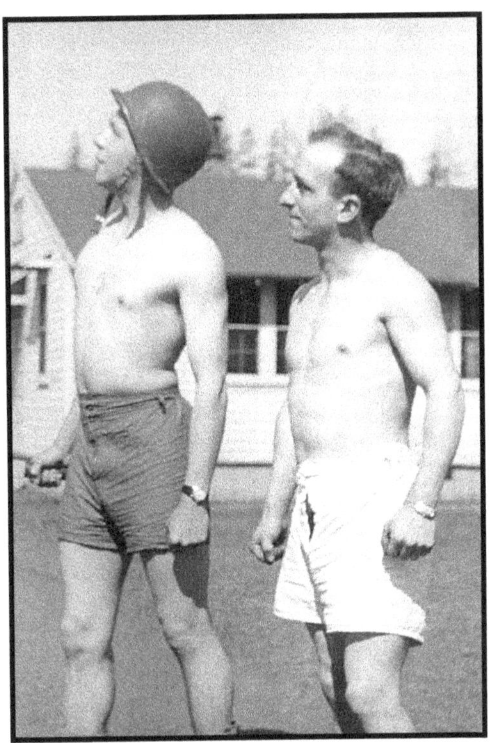

Clowning around in front of the barracks. On the back of one of the photos, he writes, "Anything for a laugh."

it now that our outfit is pretty hot. In other words, we are ready to ship out and probably will inside of the next month or two. But I hope you won't worry about me, because it will be a long time yet before I'll see any smoke… After all, there is only one thing sure about the Army, and that is the unpredictable.

April 25, 1944: Today we took a 20-mile hike, and tonight I find myself a little tired and stiff. We marched from 7:30 until about two or later. Then we had our lunch and supper in the field. The weather for the last couple of days has been pretty bad. Lots of rain accompanied by a cold spell.

May 4, 1944: Not much new or interesting has happened… The most important, I believe, is the fact that I'm still around Fort Lewis… Our orders read that we were supposed to have pulled out of here last Tuesday, the 2nd. But for reasons unknown to us, everything was cancelled. And we are now expecting to leave on a 24-hour notice. It may be a few days, weeks or maybe longer, although the "thinkers" around here don't believe so. At any rate, events are pretty uncertain.

5 Helpful Hints

On March 22, 1944, he wrote to his younger brother, Earl, who was preparing to join the army soon, offering some advice.

"Well, brother," he writes, it won't be long now until you're away from the life of ease and comfort. And at first it won't be a hell of a lot of fun. But after you have been in awhile, it won't be too bad. Just the same, you know as well as I do, that there is no place like home.

Here's a list of five "hints" he put at the conclusion of his letter:

1. Don't forget to write the folks often.

2. If you catch K.P. at the reception center when you fall out in the morning, stay as far back to the rear as possible. They usually pick the front ones for the washing of dishes, tables and floors…In general, make yourself scarce.

3. Don't let those PFCs at Custer bother you too much. They are supposed to act tough. Only you know as well as I do that they deserve to have their face pushed in. But don't do it.

4. Remember this: Don't volunteer for anything at anytime. If they want you, they will pick you. But don't volunteer.

5. Again, write the folks often.

As for your advice on drinking and women, you don't have to worry about me. I've learned my lesson about drinking, and as for as women, there is one particular one that is keeping my mind busy nowadays. So I guess that solves your problem.

- Letter to mother, June 5, 1944, Fort Lewis, Washington

He faces a long train ride, but indicates he can't reveal his final destination.

June 5, 1944: In your last letter, moms, you asked if I had any more news about my leaving. Well, I'm afraid I have. All I can say is that we are going for a train ride before the week is through. So if you don't get my mail for awhile, please don't worry. The reason will be that I will be riding around the country and it will be darn near impossible to write.

June 14, 1944: By now I suppose you know that I have finally reached my temporary destination, and about time.

His younger brother Earl, who joined the Army in the spring of 1944, about a year after my dad enlisted.

You remember how long you thought Earle's ride was, well he had it easy. I myself had six days and nights of it, or approximately 140 hours of traveling…Toward the end of it, the trip proved to be pretty boring for all.

To break the monotony, we either played cards, read anything we could lay our hands on, slept or, twice a day, they had half-hour stops in towns. When that happened, we all got off the train and either had calisthenics or a short hike. Believe me, it was a welcome relief to get off and get some fresh air and exercise.

June 17, 1944: Since we have come up here, most of our training has been confidential, and we are not allowed to talk about it. But I can say that we are kept busier than any other time that I have been in this outfit.

June 25, 1944: I'm sorry that I haven't written you for the last four of five days, but we have been so busy that when the day is through, I don't feel like writing letters. What with the two ten-mile hikes we had this week, KP, details at the warehouse, kitchen and hospital, guard duty and shots, plus inspections and a few other things, we are kept pretty busy.

August 29, 1944, France: When you mentioned just coming in from a nice swim, I just thought how nice it would be to be back there [at the cottage]. Right now, I would like to take a swim in an old swamp hole and get rid of a little of this corruption on me. The last time I washed up good was a week ago, and that was in a little stream that was colder than hell. When I did come out of it, I was just numb. For the rest of the time, I keep clean with the help of a little water in my helmet. But it's damned little and about all you can do is wash from face and hands in it…

By the way, moms, you were asking me if I needed any money. Well, thanks a lot but I have plenty. The reason is that there is no way for us to spend it over here. All our cigarettes, tobacco, gum, candy, soap blades, etc. are donated. Even our haircuts are done by guys in the outfit. As for the towns, they have nothing to sell anyway.

September 8, 1944: Well, I just moved again. There I was a few minutes ago, sitting next to a big log fire, nice and warm when all of a sudden it starts to pour. So here I am in my pup tent shivering to beat hell. Sherman sure was right when he said "War is hell." But even at that I guess I've got no right to complain. As compared to a lot of guys, I've got it pretty damn soft.

P.S. Just got back from trading with the French people. Got three dozen eggs for nine men — not bad.

Note: Hopefully, he didn't actually trade the men!

September 16, 1944: Say moms, do you remember when I was home how I used to have my pants pressed about every time I wore them, and that if I got my shirt a little spotted, I had to have a new one? Well, I've changed a little since then. Yesterday was the first time in darn near a month and a half that I had to change my O.D.s [olive drabs, so called because of the color of the uniform]. Boy they were so darn dirty that I had to tie them down at night so they wouldn't run away. At present, I'm sitting around in a pair of freshly cleaned and pressed O.D.s, just waiting to go out plowing in the mud again.

P.S. Would you please enclose some Aunt Jemima pancake flour, ready-mixed or prepared, some strawberry jam, canned butter and some pepper? Also a small jar of mustard. Thanks a lot.

October 5, 1944: Last Tuesday we had our first shower since arriving in France. Boy was it ever good. Besides that, we were able to go in swimming in an indoor heated pool, really the cat's ass.

October 15, 1944: Here it is 2:15 p.m. and I've been up since 3 a.m. this morning. I guess it sounds hard to believe, me being up that early, but duty called and I had to walk guard from 3:30 to 6:30, and it is now too late to lay down because I'm on guard in another hour.

October 28, 1944: Tonight I took my Saturday night bath. Remember when we lived in Montana and had to use tubs to bathe in? Well, that's just what I did tonight. It was a tight fit as you can understand, but it was worth it. Now I've got on all clean clothes and feel a little more at peace with the world.

January 4, 1945: I was one of two guys chosen to go on a four-day pass to Nancy [a town in France]. Boy, it was really a surprise to me that I could be so lucky. The morning before I left, I had my first shower in better than two months. That itself was great but at 12:30 the first sergeant came down and told me to be ready to leave by 1 o'clock for Nancy.

Honest, honey, if you'd care to see a little excitement, you should have seen me getting ready. Here I was, needing a shave and needing clean clothes. But I got a lot of cooperation. While I was shaving, one of the guys dug out my duffle bag and got my clean ODs, another put new laces in my shoes, another packed my toilet articles, and the rest filled my wallet. After raising a sweat and plenty of confusion, I took off on about a 100-mile trip.

February 20, 1945: The day before yesterday I received the box addressed to Frenchy [a dog they picked up], but I'm sorry to say that the little devil is lost. And boy, old Dick T. really raised hell. He was so mad when he found out about it that I thought he was going to knock the truck over. But we've got plans to pick up another one and this one isn't going to get lost.

April 4, 1945, Germany: Since my last letter to you I have been kept pretty busy. In fact, today is the first time in two weeks that I haven't had to go to the field. And believe me, it sure felt good to lie around here with nothing to worry about except probably the idea of missing chow…

This afternoon, Toady [an Army buddy] and I got ourselves a crew cut hair job. And it sure feels good not to have to comb it again for awhile. But the real reason I had her clipped is that I lost my comb

21st Birthday, Army Style

Well, people, it's finally happened. Two days ago, I became a man after 21 years of hard struggling, and to be truthful, I'm not too happy about it. Although it does have its advantages, such as it will now enable me to walk into a nightclub, order a drink, and still have a clear conscience.

But in all seriousness, it doesn't seem possible that I'm now 21. Hell, it just seems like a short while ago that I was celebrating my 16th birthday over on Hawthorne, and the big dinner you had for me. What a difference that birthday was than the one I had a couple days ago. Then the family was all together.

This year I had a bunch of swell guys around but they can never take the place of your family, and for dinner I had a can of C-rations. What irony, eh Dot?

As far as celebrating goes, I didn't do much of that. One thing, I got the day off and was allowed to lie around and clean up. And when the fellows came back from work, they had five gallons of beer that they bought for my birthday.

And, of course, as on all birthdays, I took a hell of a beating. Between rolling in a snowbank and rolling on the floor, I was well congratulated, and won't forget it for quite awhile.

- January 8, 1945

and I hated to be always borrowing. Besides, when it starts to get warmer, it will be just a lot of bother…

Say, I don't believe I've told you about my latest dog. He's a German short-haired pointer, and as Dad will tell you, he's quite a dog. He's about a year and a half old, brown and white in color and when he's on his hind legs he can put his paws on my shoulders. He also weighs about 75 pounds, so you can see that I've picked up a good-size one this time.

His name is Jerry (named after the Krauts) and is friendlier than all get out. I've only had him about a week and a half and so far he's left twice, only to come back the next morning. I suppose I'll lose him, because that's the way with life in the Army, but I've got hopes of keeping him for awhile yet.

At night he sleeps beside my bedroll, and the only trouble I've had yet is that he tries to push me off in the middle of the night. When he's at his worst is early morning. Then he wants out and goes to all extremes to get me up. Usually it's by licking my face, pulling my hair and sticking his large head between my blankets. As for his appetite, well, we don't talk about that.

[May 2, 1945] I don't believe I told you before but we were issued our ETO ribbons with two battle stars. They were for the battle of France and for the battle of Germany.

Note: The European-African-Middle Eastern, or ETO, ribbon with battle stars is awarded to members of the armed forces for their participation in a specific battle or campaign during World War II.

Chapter 3
Things That Go Bang

He writes about rifles, carbines, bazookas, torpedoes, ammunition, target practice, maneuvering a battle course, striving for high scores on the firing range — even blowing up some old cars and trucks for practice.

April 22, 1943: At 12:30, we went out on the rifle range and shot the three-hundred-yard course. I shot a 147 out of a possible 200. I'm improving a bit. We got back about five. Since we were so late, we didn't have to stand retreat.

June 6, 1943: Yesterday we were out on the firing range, shooting the carbines, and were they ever nice to shoot. Even if you can't hit anything with them. Dad, you ought to see them, and I think you could have a lot of fun with one out at the lake. They are only 35 inches long and weigh five pounds, eight ounces when fully loaded. The magazine holds 15 rounds and you can shoot it as fast as you can pull the trigger (semi-automatic). The accurate range is 150 yards, but you can hit a target at 300 yards with good conditions.

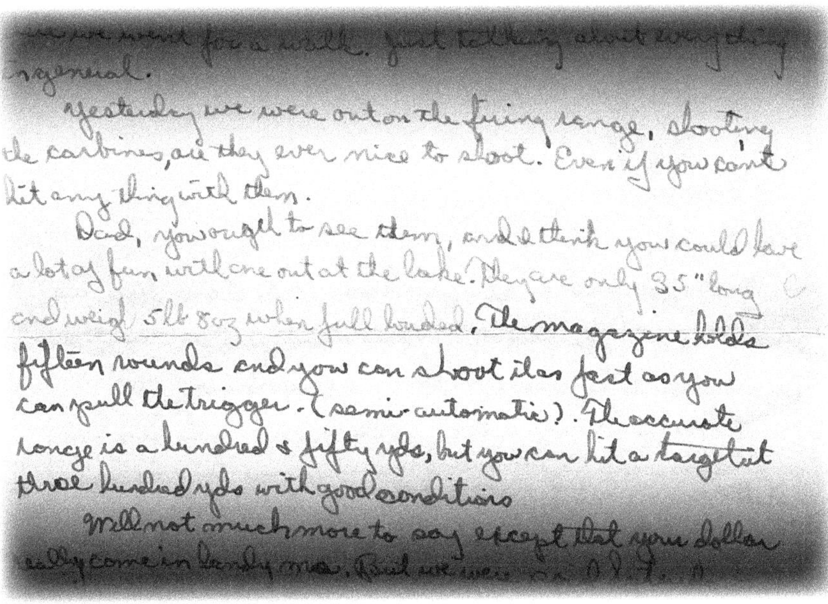

June 20, 1943: This Monday we are to go over the battle course. That's the one you have probably read about. You know, traveling 100 yards on your stomach and back with a 30-caliber machine gun over your head.

July 9, 1943: Starting Sunday we are going out in the field for seven days. While out there we will fire the carbines again, and we have to qualify with a 135 out of 200 to have any privileges around here. Also, we will practice with the guns, maybe get a chance to fire them. At least I hope so.

July 22, 1943: Yesterday morning we went out to the field for rifle and carbine practices… In the use of the carbine, I shot 169, which is sharp shooter range. With the 30-caliber rifle, I got a sore shoulder. Them damn things kick like a horse.

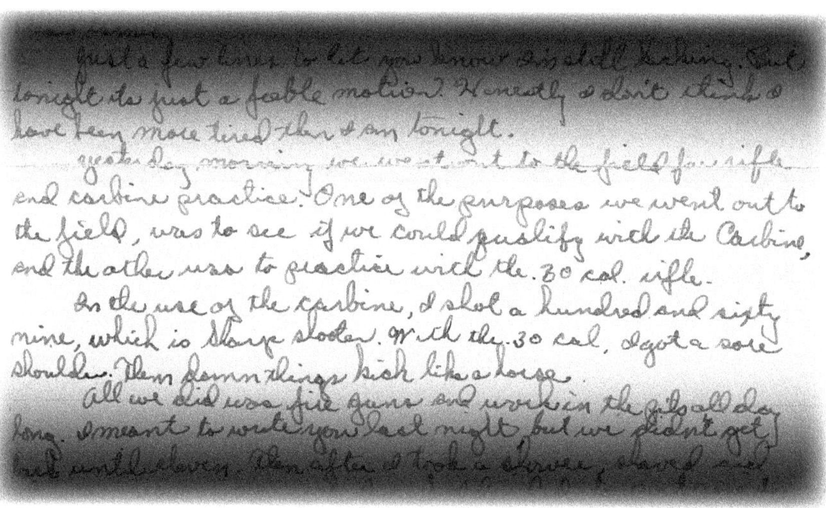

August 18, 1943: This morning we were given a practical demonstration in booby traps and personal mines. You probably have heard of them. It was all very interesting.

February 2, 1944: Monday I had to go out to the rifle range for practice. We had 60 rounds, and out of a possible score of 300, I got 287. They told me it was d_ _ _ good.

February 4, 1944: In the afternoon, we went to a bazooka exhibition and after pulling a few strings, I was allowed to fire five rounds. Believe me, that gun really packs a wallop.

April 16, 1944: For the past week I have been kept fairly busy, what with the work in the field and having one day of work in the ordinance depot. At that depot, all the ammunition for the large guns and small arms is stored. And they have plenty. Our job was to help load a boxcar with 155 shells and boxes of 30-caliber shells. The 155s alone weigh a hundred pounds. After lifting them all day a person is a little tired when he hits his bunk.

April 20, 1944: The reason we were awakened so early was so that we would be able to go out to the firing range and watch the big guns fire. A few were the 105s, but most of them were 155s, commonly called the "Long Tom," used mostly in Italy, and firing a shell weighing 96 pounds.

Boy, dad, it was really a sight. They had 60 guns firing at once, the largest group ever to fire at Fort Lewis. We were standing on a hill about seven miles ahead of the guns, watching the targets below. After seeing those shells explode, one wonders how anything lives through it.

For targets they were using old wrecks of cars. And they really knocked the hell out of them. After they were through firing, all that was left was scrap metal scattered all over the county…

Tonight, when we came in, we were issued some new equipment. They gave us new cartridge belts and two carriers for our ammunition clips for the carbine. The carbine clip holds 15 rounds each, so with four clips and one of the carbine, a fellow carries plenty of fire power.

Tomorrow the schedule calls for a field exhibition on the Bangalore torpedo and other mines, both personal and anti-tank. It should prove pretty interesting because the engineers are giving it and they have a few old trucks to blow up for us.

Chapter 4
Hitting the Books

Much of the instruction he received was similar to attending college courses. There were lectures, classes in geometry and algebra — and homework, which he loathed. Most of his classes focused on land surveying, which he found interesting and hoped might be helpful in a civilian career later, and telephone communications, which he enjoyed.

April 22, 1943: At 8 o'clock we went to a lecture. It was about our South American allies, and how much help we can expect from them. Then we went to classes from 9 to 12 and then had chow. The classes are interesting and we have some swell instructors. For the most part, they are officers and have seen action in this war.

April 30, 1943: I have just finished my homework and tomorrow we have a test in Geometry and Algebra. Also, this noon we had a two-hour test in Survey… Boy, my new work is interesting. The other morning, we had telephone communications. There were 12 of us fellows and I had charge of six of them and one telephone. All we did was lie in the woods and I gave orders back to headquarters and bossed the other fellows. More fun.

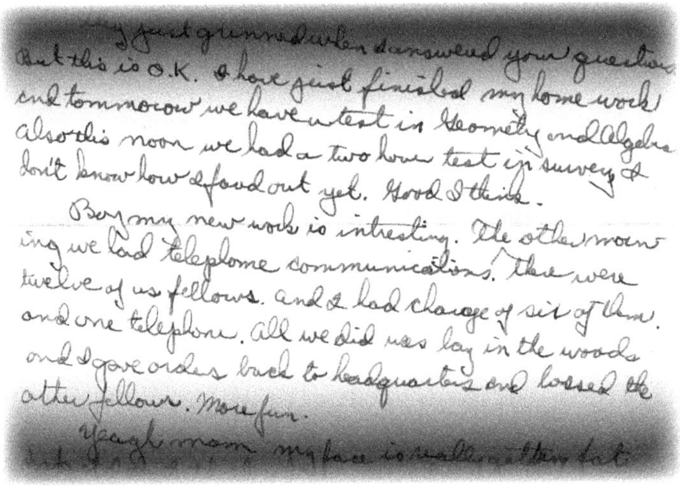
I just grinned when I answered your question
But this is O.K. I have just finished my home work
and tommorow we have a test in Geometry and Algebra
Also this noon we had a two hour test in survey I
don't know how I found out yet. Good I think.
Boy my new work is intresting. The other morn
ing we had telephone communications. there were
twelve of us fellows. and I had charge of six of them.
and one telephone. All we did was lay in the woods
and I gave orders back to headquarters and bossed the
other fellows. More fun.
Yeagh mom my face is [illegible]

May 7, 1943: All I do now is study and more study. I get so fed up with it that I would like to throw the whole thing out and get in a gun battery or mule pack where you don't have to go to school for 10 weeks.

May 11, 1943: Not much new has happened since my last letter, except that I spend most of my free time studying and trying to learn something. By the way, Dad, for the last four weeks, I have been learning Survey and how to read a level and transit. Also to measure distance and to turn angles with them. So it might help me out when I get out of this, don't you think?

June 2, 1943: Schooling goes on as before, with an extra two hours of study at night. Believe it or not, but they are trying to teach me to read maps and air photos. Impossible, I call it.

April 10, 1944: Lately we haven't been doing much except the same old job. But we are now having a few more indoor classes. Most of the schooling is on Survey so it isn't too bad. And today I had my first chance to fire the .45 revolver. They sure are a sweet gun. The only trouble is that I need a lot of practice. When I fire now, I'm usually shaking so bad that I can hardly keep the target in the sights.

May 4, 1944: Today we didn't do much except that I had to run a movie projector all morning long. The films were Directing Artillery Fire, Slicing Communications Wires and How to Recognize Enemy Vehicles. In the afternoon we had one hour of lecture and the rest of the afternoon off for athletics.

Chapter 5
Recreation and Leisure

Candy, cigarettes and trips to town were regular features of letters describing the enjoyable aspects of Army life.

Circa 1943: Tuesday night I'm going to a party given for our Battery F. About 200 of us guys and about 125 WACs. All eats and soft drinks free plus dancing. More fun. I'm really beginning to like this life. All you have to do is get it in your head that you have a job to do and there is no getting out of it.

April 18, 1943: Last night after lights were out, about eight of us guys ganged around two of our bunks and had a little party. When Slim and I were in town, we had bought a half-pound of four different kinds of candy and a couple pounds of cookies. Some of the other guys had fruit and the rest furnished the cigarettes. We had a small radio and all we did was argue about the country, wages per hour and all the subjects that we didn't know anything about. It lasted until about 11:30 when everything was gone. Boy, I really enjoyed myself.

April 22, 1943: I didn't do much on Sunday. All I did was write about 14 letters and five cards, went to a show that night and just laid around. It costs too much to go to town.

April 29, 1943: Last night I went roller skating with four other fellows. And did we have a swell time.

May 9, 1943: Slim and I had dinner in town. We had barbecued tenderloin pork with mashed potatoes and gravy, apple pie and coffee. Also fruit punch. After that, we took in a show called Manilla Calling, visited the USO later and got back to camp at 10:15.

May 11, 1943: Sunday I didn't do anything but write letters all afternoon. In the evening, I got ambitious and took my rifle apart and cleaned, oiled and polished it. Then I shined my mess kit and polished my shoes. Also did some more studying. In our barracks we have a swell time. All we do is screw around and have a good time. You won't believe it, but now they play music to us over the PA system. That is, of course, after supper. I guess they are trying to spoil us.

May 16, 1943: Today I have been very lazy. This morning, I slept in until seven-thirty. Got up and ate breakfast: six pancakes, three cups of coffee and two oranges. Then I came back and crawled back into my bed and read the paper. Finally, I got up, showered and went to church. Then I spent the day fooling around with Willy K and Slim.

My dad, at right, stands next to his buddy, Willy Kurkowski, at Fort Sill. On the back he writes, "Still rookies."

Going to the show now, will write more later on…

Well, here I am again. Gee, Smitty, tonight I really missed you. For some reason, it didn't seem right going to a show with a bunch of fellows, minus you. The picture tonight was Crash Dive with Ty Power. And it was really good. Lots of action, and it was technicolor to boot. About that picture, Slightly Dangerous," I saw it and thought it was swell. How about the time he was telling her supposed father about her [episodes of] amnesia? When he came walking in her bedroom and she smiles and says, "Hello, who are you?" I thought I'd die.

May 21, 1943: While we were in town we stopped at the USO just to look at the magazines, listen to music and eat ice cream and candy. When leaving I happened to notice some photographs on the wall. I went over to look at them and, sure enough, my picture was there. It showed me dancing with some girl. I was really surprised.

May 23, 1943: About 2:30 in the afternoon, Slim and I went to town… All we did was go around sightseeing and window shopping. We later went to the show and saw China [a war/adventure film starring Alan Ladd]. Boy, I really liked it. And last night I saw The More the Merrier. Another good picture. We also had dinner in town. After that, we went over and sat down on the courthouse lawn. Was it nice. I guess we would do anything for the change — just to get away from the routine of Army life for awhile.

June 6, 1943: This afternoon, and in fact the rest of the day, was pretty full of experiences. Slim, two other fellows and myself went riding for an hour, then into town for some refreshments. There I bought myself a new watchband and a cap. I needed both of them pretty bad. After we finished, we went swimming for a couple of hours, then to a show and saw "Pittsburgh," and after that had a <u>big steak</u> dinner.

July 5, 1943: Here I am, finally located in a new home, at least that's what I am going to have to call it for some time. The place is Camp Roberts, California… Friday noon we left Fort Sill and traveled straight through until Sunday night at nine. All the way down we had Pullman cars and swell meals, besides lots of magazines to read.

We had a swell trip. We traveled through five states: Oklahoma, Texas, Arizona, New Mexico and California. And to top it off, we rode our last leg of the journey along the Pacific Ocean, and believe it or not I saw real orange trees…

The ocean is only 12 miles from our camp, and the camp furnishes us with transportation to go swimming on Sundays…

One thing about out here is that we have the damnedest weather you ever saw. In the day it's so hot you can hardly breathe and at night it's so cold that you have to wear a jacket, and then you are still cold. But even in the hottest weather we have a nice cool ocean breeze. And is it ever nice.

October 2, 1943: In answer to your question about Shanty Town, I must say I haven't seen it yet. In fact, it's been almost a month since I have been to town. But last night I did see Girl Trouble with Don Ameche and Joan Bennett. It was an old picture but I hadn't seen it before, so it was OK. The main thing was we got a few laughs out here, and that's what counts.

January 4, 1944: On New Year's Day, a couple of us fellows were invited to a ranch for dinner. It seems as if the rancher raised hogs and had a batch of young ones around four weeks old. Well, C.U., that's the guy, finally had enough to drink that he bought one. The rest of the afternoon, he paraded it through the streets, up and down bars, in restaurants and in the USO. It really caused a sensation. When we got back from town everyone in our tent was asleep, so C.U. put the pig in bed with one of the fellows. Did he ever jump when it started to snort.

At present we are keeping him in a little cage outside of the tent and are feeding it milk and vegetables with a little coal dust for seasoning. And as for a name, we are calling him Porkie Jr., or just

Junior for short…Right now he's really cute, but I'm afraid after he puts on a hundred or so pounds, he will be a little of a bother.

February 20, 1944: Last night after finishing work, I dressed up in my best duds, and took off for the dance in Olympia [Washington]. With me went two other fellows, and when we got there. we met about 10 others. So you can see, we had quite a crowd. But with that gang, we really had a time. Everyone was full of the devil, and we really raised hell. In fact, we drove the bouncers and chaperones nutty. I did quite a bit of dancing, and met a number of female WOLVES. But mom, they don't interest me in the least. They are alright to dance with but that's as far as it goes. Besides, there is only one female that <u>interests</u> me.

April 10, 1944: This evening I went to a show and saw the picture on how the WAFS were formed. I liked it quite well myself.

Note: The WAFS, or Women's Auxiliary Ferrying Squadron, was formed in September of 1942. It was later merged into the Women Airforce Service Pilots, or WASPs.

April 20, 1944: I haven't done much of anything tonight, mostly just lying around, reading the newspapers and listening to the radio. I went down to the PX awhile back with a few of the fellows and had a small brew, but it didn't taste very good, so I gave up.

April 25, 1944: Saturday noon I took off from camp with Roberts and stayed at his place until 2 o'clock Monday morning. And every minute of it was swell.

But the best part was Mrs. Roberts, his mother, made my favorite pie for me. Lemon for me and apple for her son. Besides that, she gave up her bed for me to sleep in. A big innerspring mattress with crisp, cool sheets. You can talk about your nice people but I doubt if you can beat them.

June 25, 1944: Last Wednesday, Roberts and I got a pass for ourselves, and went into New York City on a sightseeing tour. While in town we stopped over by Carnegie Hall, Radio City, Rockefeller Center, plus a few more. We also went up in the Empire State Building. What a building, in fact it's 1,200 feet high. When you're at the top you can see most of the city in the daytime, and at night it's really beautiful.

Finishing up there, we went out and grabbed a cab and shot up to Dempsey's, where we ran into a couple of the guys. From there we went out to see the bright lights, and believe, me, we saw many of them.

August 2, 1944: Well, pops, I sure was surprised to get a letter from you because they are usually few and far between… Tonight we've got the radio going full blast. It sure reminds me of home, especially The Bob Hope Show. It just finished and The Chesterfield Hour is now on. Remember when I used to play it at home all the time? Especially when you wanted to hear the news. Boy, those were the good old days. You know I really miss those arguments we used to have. Some of them were really corkers.

Note: My dad arrived at Utah Beach in Normandy August 18, 1944, about 10 weeks after D-Day. Good timing! D-Day marked the start of Operation Overload, the code name for the Battle of Normandy, which lasted until August 30.

August 19, 1944, France: This afternoon, Roberts and I went over to a USO show, and it turned out to be pretty good. There were only about five or six performers but they put on a fair show of dancing, singing and cracking jokes.

October 15, 1944: Last Saturday we had sort of a field day here in town. What started it off was that we got the day off. About 2 in the afternoon the Red Cross Clubmobile came by and served coffee and doughnuts. And they were really good. One of the girls was from New York and after convincing her that we were practically neighbors, I had three cups of coffee along with six doughnuts. They also had a Victrola and some of the latest records.

Note: The Red Cross Clubmobile Service, created during World War II, was staffed by Red Cross volunteers, sometimes referred to as "Clubmobile girls."

Later on, a truck went into town for showers, and while there, we went swimming in the heated pool, and later on we went out and had a few cognacs washed down with the same amount of beer.

November 7, 1944: Yesterday I went into town on a pass with Roberts and we had a pretty good time. In fact, offhand, I'd say it was wilder than hell. There wasn't a lot to do except do a little sightseeing and have a few drinks. While were in town, we stopped in an old Catholic cathedral. It was really beautiful, and one can hardly imagine a building of that size in times when they had no machinery like they have today…

After a dinner with wine, we were feeling a little happy and did some screwy things. I guess the worst was when we went into a store for women and tried to buy a brassiere size 44 for a guy back in camp. We are always kidding him about how big he is and I figured that such an item would be the crowning touch. But they wanted about $14 for them, so now Niemie has to do without. But talk about laughing and raising hell. All those people in the store were laughing their tails off and I was serious about the whole thing.

January 2, 1945: Last month I really got a good deal out of the Army. It was a four-day pass to Nancy [a town in France] and I really had a time. There were only two guys out of the battery who went and I was one of the lucky ones. It was supposed to be a "rest camp" for combat soldiers, but I ran myself into the ground seeing the sights. Here's how it worked:

We arrived around five o'clock and as soon as we checked in, they took our guns and pistols and them down to the ordinances to be cleaned. Next, we were shown to our rooms, which were canvas cots about 10 to a room. Besides the cots, there was a big table loaded down with magazines, of which we see very few.

> *But the best part was the meals. Believe it or not, moms, but we actually ate non-GI food and ate it off real plates and out of real cups. But this takes the cake. You might find it hard to believe, but they had women waiting on us. At first I could hardly believe it, but after giving them the once over, it sure was OK with me.*
>
> *-January 2, 1945, at a four-day "rest camp" for combat soldiers in Nancy, France*

After we found our rooms, they took us out to the supply room and issued us a complete outfit of clean clothes and toilet articles.

As for amusement, there was much to do. In the morning breakfast was from 7:45 to 8:45, which alone was a surprise. Then from 10 to 12 the showers were open, as was the swimming pool, which was heated and really nice. At 10 the PX opened and we were able to buy magazines, stationery, film, canned orange juice, Coca-Cola, etc. Then dinner came at 11:30 and our passes in town started from 12 noon till nine at night, which is when the curfew came into effect. But the captain in charge told us not to worry if the MPs picked us up. If they did, he'd get us out or else he'd be down in there with us. And he really kept his word (I should know).

In the evenings if a guy didn't want to go out, they either had a movie or a dance (with a real woman for each guy). I was to one dance and had a good time. The babes have learned the American steps and most of them can understand a little English. One of the movies I saw was When Hearts are Young and Gay. Besides the movies and dances, they had a library or music room with records and radio and a day room. So you can see that a guy had plenty to do.

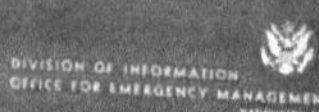
They've got more important places to go than you!...
Save Rubber
CHECK YOUR TIRES NOW
WALTER RICHARDS
DIVISION OF INFORMATION
OFFICE FOR EMERGENCY MANAGEMENT
WASHINGTON D.C.

Chapter 6
Food and Drink: Traditional Fare, K and C Rations, and Beer

When he writes about the meals he enjoys, the array of food sounds similar to what most Baby Boomers ate as children. For a closer look at food from that era, check out Betty Crocker's Picture Cookbook, published in 1950.

April 22, 1943: We got two swell meals today. Boy, they were really good. At lunch we had hot chocolate and believe it or not we had strawberry shortcake with real whipped cream for dessert. That is besides our big meal. Tonight we had filled cookies and peaches. That stuff would really raise cane with your ration book, I bet.

April 27, 1943: We get plenty to eat and some of the best. And I bet we have more of some food than you get at home. Mostly, meat is served twice a day and Fridays we usually have fish for one meal. It's really good. Grapefruit or oranges for breakfast. And we have all kinds of peaches, tomatoes, lettuce, carrots, potatoes and radishes, and raisins in our cake and cookies.

May 7, 1943: Believe it or not, yesterday I had a bowl of strawberries for breakfast, besides some more on my cereal, and in the afternoon, we had strawberry shortcake with whipped cream. It doesn't seem possible, does it?

August 18, 1943: Tonight, Johnny T. and I went over to the theater and saw a swell musical play. After that we stopped in at the service club and had a chocolate malted and a couple pieces of apple pie. It was really delicious.

October 2, 1943: This morning I slept til eight, and it sure felt good. I then got up and had my breakfast, which consisted of six large pancakes, smeared with large hunks of butter, and covered with jam; also four large strips of bacon and three cups of coffee. So you can see that my appetite hasn't been impaired.

By the way, you were saying that it was getting quite hard for you to get eats. Well, that's one trouble we don't have. Last night we had steaks, and as for butter, we have so much of it that the cooks even use it to fry in.

I've just finished eating supper and it was fairly good for a change. We had spaghetti and meatballs, mashed potatoes, tomatoes, beets, bread and butter and coffee, with cookies for dessert.

November 21, 1943: After looking over the town [Tacoma, Wash., following a furlough] a bit, we went in and had a big dinner. Our order was T-bone steak, French fries, salad, pie and coffee. Not bad, but it sure can't compete with your cooking… Now I want one more word before I sign off for the night, and that's to Mom. I want to say that your turkey dinner was the best meal I have eaten since I left for the Army. It was perfect. If anyone could beat it, I would like to know who it is, then I'll bet 10 to one yours was better.

April 16, 1944: This morning (Sunday) I woke up around eight o'clock on my own free will, if you can believe that. I then got up and washed and strolled over to the mess hall, where I fried up a mess of eggs and sausage and toast with hot coffee. If I must say so myself, I do make the best toast around here.

Note: It appears he may have missed the regular breakfast time and was allowed to cook himself a meal.

June 5, 1944: Sunday I got a guy to take my place on KP for supper and left for Seattle around 3:30. Roberts and his family

were expecting me for supper, but I didn't get in until around 6.
By that time, they had already eaten supper. Anyway, Mrs. Roberts
saved my dinner and was it ever good. She had a large roast of beef,
mashed potatoes, peas, carrots, turnips, lettuce and tomato salad,
and light brown gravy. For dessert she had a chocolate cake and a
white one with fresh strawberries with coffee, and I really stuffed
myself. You know, moms, that Mrs. Roberts is one of the nicest
persons I know. Really swell, and it seems as if she can't do enough
for me.

June 14, 1944: As for eating [while on the train after leaving
Fort Lewis in preparation for shipping out], we were pretty lucky
and didn't have to eat from our mess kits, but used paper plates.
Not only were they nice to eat from but were also easy to dispose of.
Now the eating part of it was pretty good. Three squares a day, plus
plenty of fresh fruits. And believe it or not, but every noon around
three, the cooks came through the car with these large 15 cent
Hershey bars to tide us over until supper.

June 19, 1944: Yes, I finally got to see the largest city in the
world. [Censors cut out the name of the city, but in reading the rest
of the letter, it was clear they were in the Big Apple.] And believe
me, I've had the time of my life on that pass. There were seven
of us that went in together, and after we were in town awhile, we
really got wild. Seeing as the Yanks were playing a home game, we
decided to take it in. They played a double header, and lost both
games to Philadelphia. The best part of it was that all servicemen
were admitted free, and given good seats in the grandstand located
by the right field wall. Another point was that they sold hotdogs
and beer. Well, you know us guys. What a time.

After the game was over, we all grabbed a subway and headed for
Times Square. As it was the first subway ride and we had a few
brews, we really raised Cain.

By the time we got downtown, it was around six o'clock, so after looking around awhile, we finally picked an Italian restaurant and ordered a big spaghetti dinner.

August 29, 1944, France: As for our eating situation, we aren't doing too bad. We have had about two hot meals from the kitchen and the rest have been C and K rations. Once in awhile they serve hot coffee but otherwise we get our own. Even at that I'm not losing any weight, and the rations are pretty good and filling.

> *Another thing I've tried is cognac. Our outfit got in on a trainload of cognac that was captured from Germans, dated 1907. Boy, talk about the good stuff. That stuff really had a kick to it.*
> *- September 16, 1944, France*

September 16, 1944: The time is now 1 p.m. and I have just eaten dinner. It wouldn't compare with any of your meals by a long shot, but it will do to keep me going. Our menu consisted of fried potatoes, which [came] out of a Frenchman's potato patch, beans, jam, cocoa, sugar, all of which was captured from German warehouses, and French bread.

By the way, moms, I don't believe I told you about this bread over here. Well to begin with, it's in the shape of a doughnut about a foot in diameter and weighs about three to four pounds. Heavier than hell for its size, Besides that, it seems as if it isn't baked thoroughly, which in turn makes it really tough. [What he's describing is a couronne, a type of French country bread.] In fact, if I eat much more of the stuff, I'll need a new set of molars when I get back to the States. The bread costs eight francs or 16 cents a loaf.

Since I've been over here, I've looked a little into a subject that holds a great deal of interest for dad. And as you know, dad, that subject is cold beer with a touch of good liquor. Well, dad, the Frogs over here have the right idea about beer. [Frogs is a slang term for the French.] They serve it cold like in the States. And it's quite a bit like ours except that it's sweeter.

October 28, 1944: As for eats, we are still getting hot meals, with a sprinkling of C rations when we are out in the field all day. Tonight, believe it or not, we had fried chicken. I'll admit that the chicken was darn slim. But just the same, it's the idea of the thing.

November 7, 1944: I don't know if one can call it lucky or not but we found about the only place there was in town to eat. We had roast beef, potatoes, macaroni, wine and pea soup, which was served first, and it all came to about three dollars each. It was good food and the wine was even better.

As far as the waiters, they were in style, wearing tails and even cufflinks. The strange part was the way they served the food. The first thing they did was to put out wine glasses and a quart of wine. Then they brought out the food. They had all our orders on one big platter and let us help ourselves. I don't know if that's the custom over here or it's just the shortage of help. The only thing wrong was that they rationed only one quart of wine to a customer, and there was no bread with the meal. There is such a shortage of bread here that they laid down the law that GIs are not allowed to buy it anymore. If we are caught it's a military offense.

January 2, 1945: For Christmas dinner we had turkey (lots of it), mashed potatoes, string beans, brown gravy, salad, raisin bread, real butter, coffee, dessert, Hershey's chocolate and a cigar. We had the same menu for New Year's.

January 29, 1945: Dad, remember the tea you sent? Well, the guys sure raised hell with that. They call me "Honker" once in awhile because I come from Canada, but they really put it on about me being a "Limey tea drinker." Even at that, they sure went through it fast and I wish you'd send some more…

Just got back from chow and did fairly well. We had spaghetti, boiled potatoes and gravy, bread and butter, string beans, sliced pineapple, coffee and last but not least, we had vitamin pills, which we get every night.

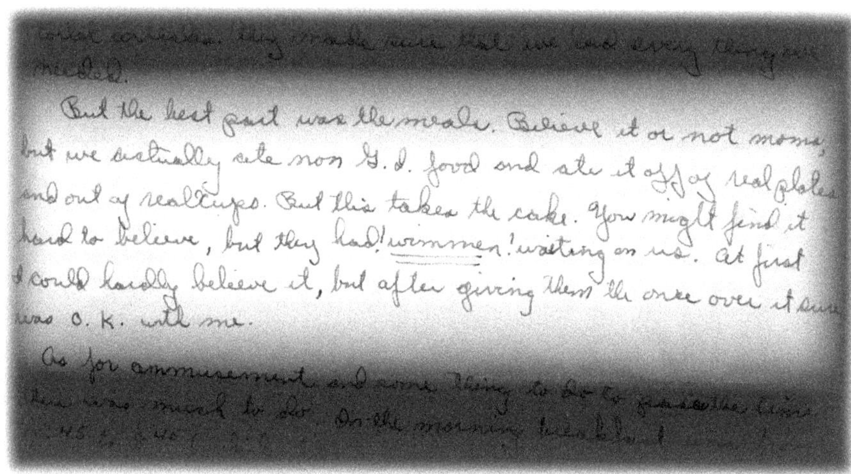

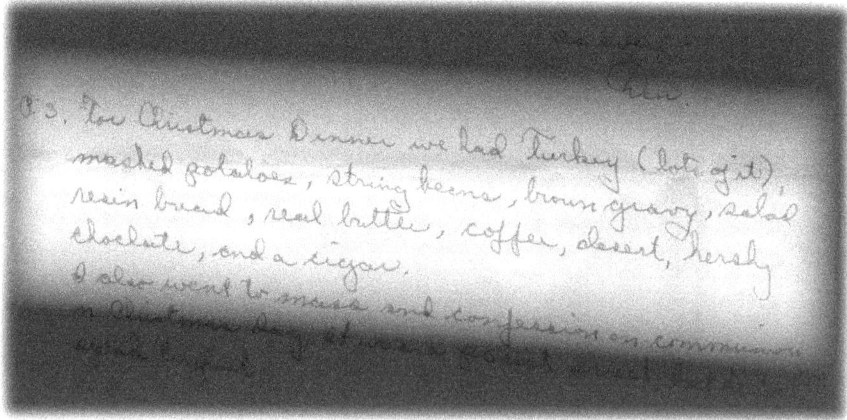

Two excerpts from a letter dated January 2, 1945, both mentioning meals he enjoyed.

Chapter 7
Smoking: That Ubiquitous Pastime
of the Forties

Smoking, along with chewing gum and eating candy, appears to be a common pastime for soldiers. Lots of the letters mention smoking — and care packages from family and friends often included cartons of cigarettes. According to the Army Historical Foundation, mini-packs of certain cigarette brands were included in the rations issued to fighting troops, a practice that ended in 1976. In addition, major tobacco companies often supplied the USO with standard packs to try to build brand loyalty.

Circa 1943: Say, Dad, it sure would be expensive for you to smoke down here. Luckies, Raleighs and all the other 15-cent cigarettes are 20 cents a pack here. But we get them for 13 cents at the PX.

April 18, 1943: I am lying in bed and smoking a cigar. Excuse the writing please.

April 22, 1943: Yes, there are some things you can send. Shaving lotion and stockings, the white wool ones. Cigarettes and everything a soldier likes, and I would still like to have a camera and as much film as you can get. It's almost impossible to get it up here. I'll be glad to pay for it. How about taking some pictures and sending them to me? I would like to see what the family looks like.

May 18, 1943: This evening I received Earle's welcome package. And boy it was swell. Everything was what I needed. At the present time I had about two razor blades left. And all my stockings are at the laundry. Also I was just about out of shoe polish. The cigarettes really brought me up. Yesterday I got a carton from Mrs. Adams and Frances, also the rosary from Mrs. Lang, which I think is beautiful. I offered the first rosary for her baby and the family.

September 8, 1944: So far, I haven't received any packages, but I am really looking forward to getting them, especially the lighter. As for the cigarettes, I can usually make out because they give us a carton about every 10 days.

January 29, 1945: By the way, moms, you were worrying about me getting enough smokes. Well, it's OK. Since November we've been getting five packs a week, plus soap, a little gum and candy. But today we got seven packs again, plus three chocolate bars, seven sticks of gum, matches and pipe tobacco. Lately I've started smoking a pipe in the evenings. [Pipes] don't work so hot in the field.

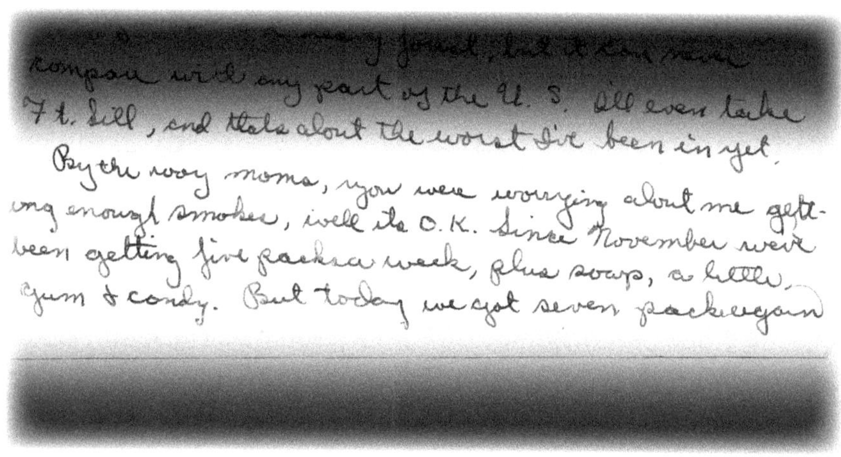

Chapter 8
Romance

My mom used to complain that my dad's letters from the Army weren't very romantic. They were mostly about what he did and where he went. But there were a few exceptions.

October 8, 1943: About six days ago I received one very nice letter and a better picture. By the way, honey, did I ever tell you that you were beautiful? If I didn't, I must have been dead or least awfully ignorant. When I showed the fellows your picture, they just whistled and made some very complimentary remarks, of which I agreed wholeheartedly.

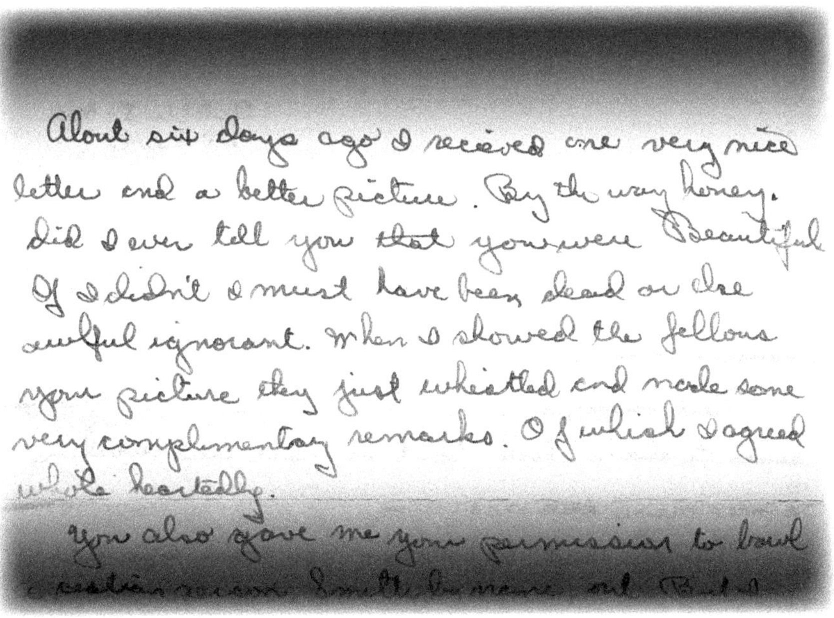

February 9, 1944: Talking about Washington, it's a beautiful place in the summer, or so they tell me. But until then it's mostly all wet. But regardless of the weather, I would give anything to see you again. Since I've had my furlough, nothing seems to satisfy me.

December 5, 1944: We've got the radio on again and Glenn Miller's band is going full blast. They've just finished playing "Tangerine" and "Moonlight Serenade," and it really makes me think of you. I'd give anything to be back there with you again.

January 4, 1945: You know, honey, I was reading over that part about you telling the folks about our escapade in Palmer Park. I can't help thinking about that without grinning. You were really the sad sack that night, but I love you more than ever for it. But seeing as you told them, I'll have to walk in backwards the next time I come to see you. What can they think of the guy that takes out their daughter, gets her tight [a slang word for drunk] and then lets her stagger around a public park? Maybe you'd better not answer that…

Say, Helen, will you send me the definition of a lady? These guys are all arguing about it and have their own opinions, but none of them satisfy me.

March 9, 1945: Boy, tonight I got a pleasant surprise, and it came in the form of a letter. And it sure was good to hear from you. On the whole, I do pretty good for myself as far as mail goes, and I sure do enjoy hearing from the rest of the world. But the ones I most look forward to are the ones you write. You know, kiddo, I really miss you and instead of it getting easier on me, it gets worse.

Chapter 9
The Value of a Dollar

In reading these letters, I was reminded of how far a dollar went in the 1940s. For example, chicken cost 59 cents a pound in 1943 and Campbell's tomato soup was advertised at 27 cents for three cans, according to OneTubeRadio.com. Of course, inflation over the years has played a big role: one dollar in 1943 is the equivalent to $15.78 in 2021.

Circa April 1943: Got paid today but after they got through taking out my insurance bonds and laundry I drew only seven bucks. Then I donated one dollar to the Red Cross. Boy, I'll have to skimp now.

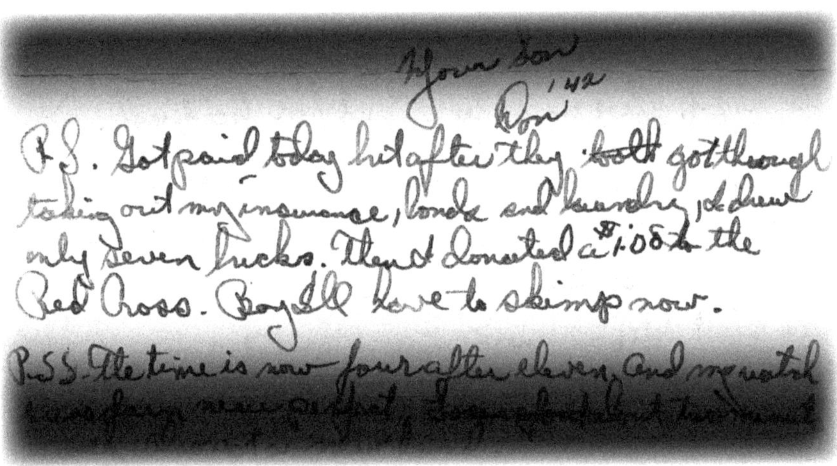

May 7, 1943: Wednesday is payday, and it sure feels good to have money in your pocket again. And that's where I am going to keep it from now on. But the temptation is pretty big to spend it. After all, you work a full month for about 35 bucks after all your deductions are made. And it really isn't very much when you figure out how much it costs to have a fairly good time here.

May 23, 1943: Dad, I got your letter today and it was swell, also the dollar came in handy. It helped pay for my shoes. The darn things cost $2.50 to get repaired — a darn crime, I call it.

June 6, 1943: Your dollar really came in handy, ma…I suppose you wonder what I spent it on. Well, I spent 85 cents for cleaning and 14 cents on cigarettes and matches. I still have a penny left.

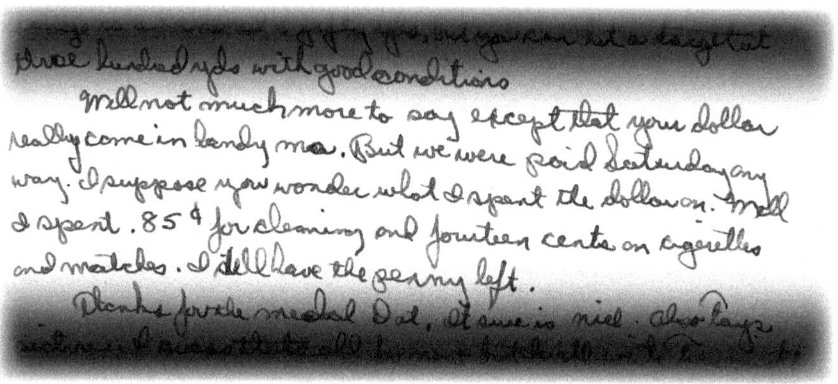

June 8, 1943: Well, ma, I got your letter today with the buck. Thanks. I didn't need it, but I will save it for something special.

April 10, 1944: Last week I made out an allotment…So starting the first of next month, I will have $25 a month taken out and sent home. What I would like for you to do is put it in the bank for me. You won't get it until around the end of May, and after the first check you will get one around the eighth of every month.

April 16, 1944: For a change I stayed in camp this weekend, but the only thing that held me back was the fact that I was on guard Saturday night. And besides that, I promised Roberts I would take his table waiting over the week so he could go home. He wanted to pay me five bucks but I settled for three. After all, he can't afford it any better than myself.

June 17, 1944: When our overseas pay comes into effect, I will be making $64.80 instead of my regular $54. And over there we should be able to get along on $15 a month. After my insurance, $25 allotment and $18.75 for a bond is taken out, I will possess the grand total of $14.55. Not much, I admit, but I believe I'll be able to get along on that.

October 2, 1944: I don't know if Helen told you or not but I finally got a rating. Last September I made corporal with about a $15 more a month raise. Over here a rating doesn't mean a hell of a lot. Back in the States it means no more KP or walking guard and fewer details, etc., but over here it just means more work with less complaining. The nicest part is more money, which will come in handy when the war is over.

October 15, 1944: P.S. Could you enclose a comb in the next letter? Over here in the larger towns they want 70 francs ($1.40) for one.

March 23, 1945: By the way, the letter from Earl had a five dollar bill included for my Christmas present. He apologized for not sending me something sooner, but he was broke, and if it wasn't for a guy paying off a bet, he wouldn't have been able to send me anything.

But believe me, that $5 sure looks good. I'm carrying it around in a celluloid case in my shirt pocket till I hit the States. Then, watch my smoke.

"OF COURSE I CAN!
Dick Williams
I'm patriotic as can be —
And ration points won't worry me!"
WAR FOOD ADMINISTRATION
Washington, D. C.

Chapter 10
Making Time for Religion

My dad was what they now call a "cradle Catholic," and he continued to practice his faith during his war years. He attended Catholic schools throughout his life, graduating from St. Rita High School (now closed) in Northeast Detroit in 1942.

As a side note, it's easy to forget how important high school was to kids of that era, many of whom had parents who never graduated from high school. In fact, my dad signed many of his letters "Don, Class of '42."

On Easter Sunday I am going on a procession. It is a pageant and you most likely have heard of them. It starts about five in the morning (sunrise). There are people who reenact the Last Supper, Resurrection and all that stuff. Oklahoma is noted for this spectacle. It lasts until about 11 o'clock. People from miles around come to watch it.

- April 1943, Fort Sill, Oklahoma

Circa April 1943: Tomorrow morning I am going to church and communion come hell or high water. I also say my prayers every night for you. I have been trying to get a rosary but it's nigh on impossible. I haven't seen any yet. Say a prayer that my pictures turn out fair, and I'll send some home.

January 4, 1944: On New Year's morn, five other fellows and myself checked out a command car and went to church in town [Tacoma, Washington]. After church, we had breakfast and then took a sightseeing tour until it was time to eat lunch. After that, we came back to camp and had a bull session for the rest of the day.

February 13, 1944: I was just at church and communion, and now feel quite a bit of an angel. If that were possible. The chaplain gave us a good strong talk, but it wasn't on the Gospels. It was this business of mixed marriages and marrying out of the church. It seems as if there has been a great deal of that happening around here and he was pretty hot about it.

Note: Mixed marriages, meaning marrying a person of a different religion, was a big issue in the 1940s but something you rarely hear about today. And it wasn't just about a Christian marrying a non-Christian. A Catholic marrying a Protestant was considered unacceptable, and it appears that's what the chaplain was referring to when he spoke of marrying "out of the church."

April 10, 1944: Today, believe it or not, I went to two masses. One was at nine o'clock in the main post chapel. The chaplain had all kinds of flowers on the altar and it really looked nice. The other was at 12:40 at our own chapel. So seeing as I wasn't doing anything important, I just wandered over. At present I feel pretty holy, but then, who wouldn't?

April 16, 1944: After eating supper, Joe Baldus and myself went to the evening mass. After mass was over, we had a special streak of holiness, so we went to confession. Later on, we met the chaplain and chewed the fat for awhile with him. He is a pretty good egg. Just a young guy that's been in the Army a short while. When and if we go [overseas], I hope he will come with us. In fact, he voiced the same opinion.

May 4, 1944: Dick is lying across from me and says for me to tell Mom that he is "looking over me like a guardian angel." He's the fellow I told you about who lives near Flint.

July 23, 1944, England: Last night they held mass and communion for us and I attended and went to Communion. This morning, I did it again, and now I feel so holy that I'm a little afraid to visit the pubs.

August 29, 1944, France: I've been getting my church schedule in for the last couple weeks. The only hard part about mass here is that the preaching [the homily] is all in French, so us guys have to sit around like a bump on a log.

A Snorting Good Time at Church

Here's an excerpt from one of his letters from Luxembourg, dated January 29, 1945.

You know how restless one gets when you've got to listen to some dry sermon, during which the priest goes right on raving?

Well, that's the way this one was, only it was all in German and we couldn't understand a word. Here he was, a little guy about five-foot-four, weighed about a 120 pounds, wore classes and was about 65 years old. He was standing up in this pulpit and you could really see that he was enjoying himself. He had a bad habit of snorting like a dog after every two or three sentences. It got so, I started to do it myself to see if it could be done and so were half the guys in my pew.

He'd shout for awhile, then whisper, all the while keeping his eyes shut. This went on for a half-hour, and during that time I thought he was going to fall out of the pulpit at least a half dozen times. So help me, he didn't open his eyes once till he was finished. I looked around and found half the people dozing off so they must have been pretty well used to him.

By the way, we sort of messed up and sat on the women's side. We got a few blank looks but, honest, can you tell me a better place to be? Yow!

October 15, 1944: Today is Sunday, and this morning I went to confession, church and communion again. This makes three Sundays in a row that I've done the same thing. It's beginning to look as if I've finally seen the light, and am leading a life of holiness (just kidding). But I really have changed a bit and I can give most of the credit to the Jerries [British slang for Germans]. So, Sister M. Joseph is back again? Well, that's where St. Rita gains something. She's alright. I'll admit she's a little rough at times, but she's always fair and willing to look at the best side of things. Tell

her I said hello and that I still think of her as the best teacher I had
in high school, even if she did try and embarrass me by calling me
the playboy of the class of '42.

November 7, 1944: As for my religious life over here, I am
doing pretty good. Last week I was to church three times. I went to
communion on All Soul's Day and to confession and communion
on Sunday. We are sure lucky because there are lots of guys that
don't get a chance to go to church at all.

January 2, 1945: I went to mass, confession and
communion on Christmas Day. It was a parish priest but he
could speak English. And on New Year's Day, Joe B. and I went
to mass. We wanted to go to confession, but the priest could only
understand a little English. So instead of hearing our confessions,
he gave us general absolution. So you can see that I haven't
forgotten my religious training.

Chapter 11
Contemporary References:
Hitler, Bob Hope and More

April 30, 1943: Tonight I am going to see Lana Turner in Slightly Dangerous.

May 31, 1943: How is your sister making out? I guess she really feels bad about Dick planning on leaving [to join the Navy]. You know, common sense tells me it isn't right after all — they were just married and now he probably has to leave. Boy, I hate Hitler and his little Jap friend.

Note: Dick is the husband of his girlfriend Helen's sister Betty.

June 2, 1943: Kay Kyser is now on the radio playing "Let's Get Lost." Boy, wouldn't I like to.

June 8, 1943: Here it is Tuesday evening and I have just heard Bob Hope and now "Red Skelton" [Skelton's radio show] is on. Those guys are nuts!

June 20, 1943: Say, Smitty, do you remember that picture Holiday Inn with Bing Crosby? Well, I saw it again tonight. Just as good as ever. And to top it off, a few moments ago, the radio was playing "Deep Purple." Solid.

Oct. 8, 1943: Well, Smitty, my faith in [the University of] Michigan is pretty low tonight. In fact, I was so sure of their team winning that I lost six bucks. Besides that I'm getting the devil razzed out of me. But such is life.

Helen, will you tell me something? Last Saturday night I was listening to Hit Parade. Frank Sinatra was singing and those women were actually moaning. Why?

December 16, 1945: Say, Dad and Mom, the radio just played White Christmas. Do you remember last year when I took both of you to the Cameo to see Holiday Inn? That was the picture with Bing Crosby.

Note: Holiday Inn was the predecessor of the 1954 film White Christmas.

June 25, 1944: Last Thursday, Roberts and I went to the show and saw Bathing Beauty with Red Skelton and Esther Williams. That was really okay, in fact, I laughed so darn much that I got cramps before the picture was half over. Not only comical but a good story and in technicolor.

Well, folks, a couple of the fellows just dragged me off to a show, "This is the Army," with Ronald Reagan and Joan Leslie, to broaden my outlook in life, or at least that's what they say. It was pretty good.

August 2, 1944: Last night Toady and I went into town for a little relaxation. We had a few bitters and then went to a show, Buffalo Bill with Joel McCrea, and it was really good.

August 19, 1944: Frank Sinatra is now singing "That's Amore" on the "Hit Parade." Pretty good.

October 15, 1944: By the way, I was just reading what Bing Crosby had to say about the troops. Boy, he really gave us a buildup. He said, "The closer you get to the front, the higher the morale. They're cleaner shaven, clothes are cleaner, they're more precise and their salutes really snap."

It may be all well and true, but he sure wasn't here to see our saluting because last week we had the hell bawled out of us by a two-star general for not throwing the "old highball." But if Bing is satisfied, so are we. Don't get me wrong. He still rates top with us but we also got a laugh out of it.

BUY WAR BONDS

Chapter 12
Health, Well-Being and Medical Care

According to the U.S. Department of Defense (defense.gov), medical improvements saved many lives during World War II. For example, service members were inoculated for smallpox, typhoid, tetanus, cholera, typhus, yellow fever and bubonic plague, depending on where they were sent. To treat bacterial infections, penicillin or streptomycin were administered for the first time in large-scale combat.

April 25, 1943: Boy, you all wouldn't believe it, but the fellows are starting to razz me by calling me "Chubby." The only thing that looks fat about me is my face, and it looks as if I may get a double chin. But it don't worry me too much. I would rather be fat than skinny. Wouldn't you?

April 27, 1943: I am in good health but to tell you the truth, I don't believe that I have ever been more tired at night as I have been in the last week and a half. And tonight is no exception. I guess it's the heat and exercise that does it…Mother, I know you worry quite a bit about me. Well please don't. After all, we have the best of medical aid. We have a mess of hospitals on the post and as many dentists. If you don't feel right in the morning, you report for sick call at 8:00 and they take you right over to the hospital.

May 21, 1943: I am fine and feeling better every day. Also, my hair is coming in and my tan is darker. But I still don't know why you don't see any changes in me, because I have gained about 20 pounds. Maybe it's that I am just getting more solid. I honestly think that this life is good for you. Regular hours for sleeping, eating and resting are the cause of it. But I can tell you that it is doing me a lot of good.

June 2, 1943: For the first time in my Army life I reported for sick call. It was just my bum leg giving out on me. I injured it during the last football season, the one I played in. The darn thing started aching and kept me awake at night. The doc gave me some salve to put on it. If it doesn't help, he is going to X-ray it. Oh, boy, I'm going to get my picture taken again.

January 21, 1945, Luxembourg: As usual, I'm later than hell in writing you and I guess I should be ashamed of myself. But the reason I haven't written you in the last couple of weeks is that I have been sicker than a dog and been spending most of my time lying flat on my back. And for the last four days I've spent my time in the hospital with a temperature as high as 103.4. And believe me I sure felt like the last rose of summer.

While I was in the hospital, I had the war pretty well made. All my meals in bed, and lots of sleep. Of course I was stuffed with pills, medicines and thermometers, but it was worth it. The doc figured I had a touch of a certain type of flu, but I'm OK now, and that's all that counts.

Got back with the gang today and felt pretty good. The only ill effects visible are that I've lost a little color and about 10 pounds. But I'll get that back soon.

March 12, 1945: As for myself, I'm feeling swell and am getting plenty to eat and lots of good rest when it's needed. About all I'm suffering from now is a skinned shin that I got from wrestling with Roberts.

Chapter 13
Care Packages,
Letters from Home, Phone Calls

Letters from home and care packages were huge morale boosters for servicemen, as they are today. My dad wasn't hesitant to ask family members to send certain items, either, and his requests were often made in a P.S. to his letters. Whatever treats he received were shared with others, so they didn't last long.

July 16, 1943: My attitude toward Army life has changed a small portion. After receiving two letters from you, two from home and one from the Adamses, my morale jumped by bounds.

April 11, 1944: It's approximately two hours after my phone call, and it sure was nice to hear all of you talking once more. It was so darn nice that I didn't have the willpower to stop running up the bill. Since I've come back, I've just laid on my back and thought over what we talked about. When I come to think about it, we didn't talk about much of anything, did we? Anyway, I really enjoyed it.

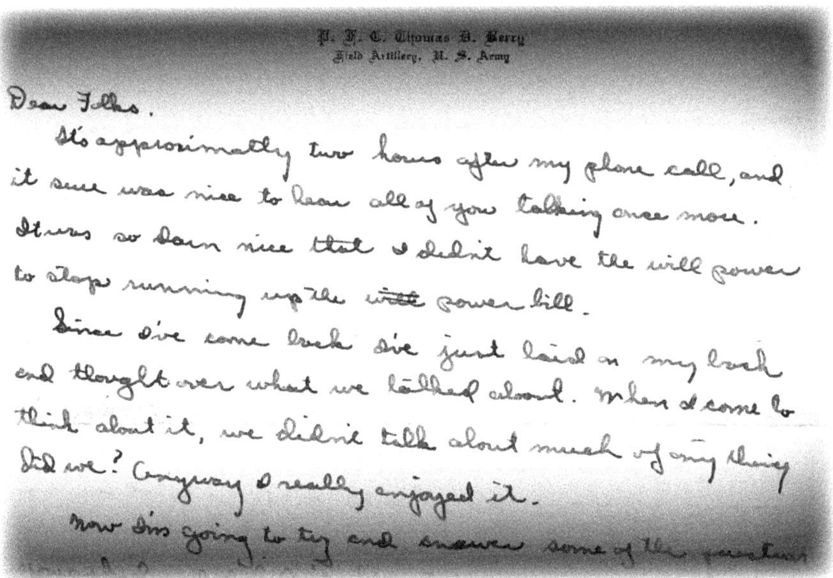

April 25, 1944: Man, oh, man, was I ever surprised last night, and it sure was a nice surprise. Around 8:30 I was called over to the orderly room to answer a phone call. At first I couldn't figure out who in the world wanted to phone me. When I did lift the receiver, who should be at the other end but Larry Urban himself. He was over at the main fort, so I dressed up, grabbed a weapon carrier and shot over on the double. It was really swell to see him once more. He was only able to stay till eleven-thirty, but we sure packed in a lot of talking in the short time we had. It seemed as if it were only yesterday that we were home together, raising hell and drinking more beer than was good for us. Our main topic was of the gossip around the neighborhood.

He seems to like the Navy quite a bit, but right now he is a little more than lonesome. I can understand, because I know how it is. Just getting off of furlough and coming back to camp is no fun.

August 13, 1944: P.S. How about some airmail stationery and candy? I need it bad.

August 22, 1944: P.S. How about some cake and cookies? It would make those rations a little more bearable.

August 29, 1944: Last Sunday we had mail call for about the first time in three weeks, and believe me, it sure was like seventh heaven to get mail from home again. Although I got only two from you, I received seven from Helen and two from Earle. It seemed like "Old Home Week" again and raised my morale 100%...

P.S. Could it be possible for you to send me some aftershave lotion, magazines, T-shirts, etc.? Thanks.

January 8, 1945: When I came back from supper tonight, I sure was in for a surprise. There were three packages from home, and the first I've received since last September. They were from Dot, Junior and Kenny, and were really appreciated.

The peanuts and candy sure tasted good, only they didn't last 15 minutes. But the aftershave lotion, shaving cream, soap, toothbrush and power, etc., are really going to come in handy, as will the sweater.

January 29, 1945, Luxembourg: Around Christmastime, I got a nice card from Roberts' mother and sisters, and a long letter. They've got pictures and cookies on the way, and told me that they would be thinking of me on Christmas, and that they missed my bull sessions at their house. A couple days ago I helped him eat a box of cookies and candy that his sisters had sent to him and me. So you can see for yourself that one meets some mighty nice people in this world…

Before I sign off, there are a few things I'd like to ask for. One of them is a good wallet with places to carry pictures. Also about three pairs of those leather gloves for work. Dad knows the kind. They are sheepskin, goat skin or something. They cost about 75 cents to a dollar a pair. The size is small or an 8. Also, how about some good novel? Of that I want you to take it from my money. You've got enough to buy for yourselves and the kids…

By the way, there is probably something that Kenny wants pretty bad now — a cap gun, truck, cowboy suit or something. What I want you to do is buy it for him and use my money. I'm not around to do it myself. If it's a bigger bike or a wagon, it's OK; in fact, it's all the same with me. I'd just like him to have what he can get.

February 4, 1945: I see that you heard from Minnesota City again, and you asked me if I remembered those days. I sure do.

I can still see myself running around with those kids form the Oaks Night Club and getting in those tomato fights we used to have. Or how about the time I put my hand through the school window and Manfred had to rush me to the hospital in Winona? I can still see myself trying my darndest to faint, and not quite succeeding. And wasn't it just about that time that Dot fell by the pump and broke her arm? Boy, we really had our troubles.

I guess what I remember most was the time Earl got mad and decided to run away. The farthest he got was to hide in the storage shed, but there you were, coaxing him to come in. Those were the days, and I wish we were all back in them again. Do you remember the time I shot Dot in the leg with my BB gun? Boy, Dad sure got mad and I guess I suffered more than she did.

February 17, 1945: Yesterday I got a short letter from Earl and learned that he has finally landed on the shores of "sunny France," only from what he claims it isn't exactly warm, in fact it's darn cold. He didn't have much to say, mainly that he was sure looking forward to seeing me.

And he sure isn't the only one. If things would turn out alright and I could find where he's staying, I'd sure look him up if he's within a hundred miles or so of me. At present, I'm really looking forward to seeing him, and hoping for the best, although just between you and me, I wish that he could stay way back there.

Note: Although they really wanted to, they never had a chance to meet up, unfortunately.

February 20, 1945: P.S. Could you send some dill pickles, red peppers and food? Dick said that the boys all love you, but would love you a lot more if you would send more food, such as sardines, soup, tuna, and oysters.

March 4, 1945: Since my last letter to you, I have received a number of letters from you, ranging from Feb. 1 through the 20th. Among them were those from Dad, Moms and Junior. And a couple nights ago I received the box of candy from Aunt Muriel. Honest, it was the best candy I've eaten since God knows when. The only trouble was that I didn't get enough for the gang, and every time I looked around, there they were, licking their chops and saying, "Don't mind if I do."

This man is your FRIEND
Canadian
He fights for FREEDOM
For additional copies write to Graphics Division, Office of Facts and Figures, Washington, D. C. . . . Specify GPO Jacket No. 455916.
U. S. GOVERNMENT PRINTING OFFICE : 1942—O

Chapter 14
Journey to Citizenship

My dad, who was born in Loretteville, Quebec, finally got his Certificate of Naturalization on March 27, 1944, while he was residing at Fort Lewis, Washington. He was 20 years old.

February 20, 1944: It's beginning to look as if I am finally going to get my citizenship papers. Thursday, I filled out an application, and had as my witnesses our battery commander and another officer from Personnel. On Friday I was taken over to the Signal Corps and had my picture taken for the papers. So this Tuesday they are to be finished, and I have been promised to get myself out of guard duty.

February 27, 1944: Well, mom, I found out some more dope on my citizenship papers. There was some mix-up, so now they want my first papers and my Declaration of Intention. The reason they want all this dope is because they want to know when I came to the States, on what train, on what route, etc.

I believe I'll get a trip to Portland, Oregon, when I take my final oath. With all expenses paid. It will be a nice little jaunt, only 137 miles from here. I enjoy a trip like that, especially if it's on the Army.

March 29, 1944: Well, Dad, as of Monday, I am now a full-fledged citizen. That's right. A real American citizen. I finally took my oath and received the papers and now feel pretty good about the whole deal.

RATIONING MEANS A FAIR
SHARE FOR ALL OF US

Chapter 15
An English Travelogue

Following are some glimpses of England, as seen through my dad's eyes. The first is a complete letter, dated July 20, 1944. On the back of one of the pages, his sister, Dorothy, includes this note to their brother Earl: "This is a letter from Don, which he asked us to send on to you. Keep it for it will be something interesting to read in future years." I doubt they ever actually looked at it in later years, although I'm sure they would have enjoyed it.

Dear Folks,

By this time, if you have received my V-Mail letters, you will know that I am now someplace in England. And to be truthful, it's pretty nice where we are stationed, although it can never compare with the States.

England is a great deal like our Northwestern states, Washington in particular. In the summer, the weather is mostly a mild climate with a few heat bursts, and in the winter, it is about the same [as in the States]. As for snow, they don't worry about it, but have plenty of rain and fog.

Honest, moms, there is some of the nicest scenery around here, especially in the country. The English people, as you know, have very little land, and what they do have, they take exceptional care of. Most of the small farms are divided from one another by hedges, and looking at them from the hilltops reminds you of a patchwork quilt. Really pretty.

What I have seen so far of the English homes, I think that in most cases they are very good. Although in many cases their homes are quite old, they look to be in fairly good condition. Since the war started, 1939 over here, the people have not been able to get paint or other accessories to improve the looks of the homes, but with what little they have, they did a great job. One thing there is a shortage of is curtains. So the people decorate the windows with flower pots and polish their windows till they really shine. And to me they look a lot better.

As for the English people, they are alright. Honestly, folks, these people over here are the friendliest ones I have yet met. Everyone you meet seems to have a pleasant smile and a good word for one. And it just seems as if they can't do enough for us. You can stop them anytime and ask them questions, which they will to their darndest try to explain and make it clear.

For the most part they are quite a bit like us, but their customs are quite a bit different than ours. I guess the best way to say it is they are quite old-fashioned.

Over here they still count their money in pounds, crowns, shillings, pence and pennies. And believe me it was really confusing at first. In fact, I'm still a little dense on the whole subject. They are also driving on the wrong side of the road with right-wheel drive, and are still riding bicycles, both young and old. Also, the favorite pastime over here seems to be walking. It's nothing to see some old gent with a mustache, wearing knickers and swinging a cane down the road.

One thing that really shows up over here is that it seems to be the fashion for everyone to push a baby carriage down the street, and it is usually loaded. As for the kids, they are the same as in any other country. Only over here, they really go for candy and gum more so than at home. Reason is that they seldom get any unless it's from the American soldier, and believe me they know it.

Another thing about England is that they know that there is really a war going on. Besides the bombing, there is the rationing, which is really strict. If people think it is tough back home, they ought to be in these people's shoes. For instance, butter is unheard of over there, they are allowed only a quarter pound of sugar a week, no gas at all unless [someone is] on government business. Then it costs 60 to 70 cents a gallon. Coffee is scarce. Kids haven't had ice cream since '39 in most cases. As for fruits, when they can get them, lemons and oranges cost about one dollar to $1.50 apiece, apples 75 cents apiece. They are allowed one egg a week when they can get them, and jam is a luxury. To get a pair of shoes, one sacrifices about a quarter of his coupons for the year on clothing. And jewelry has a 200% luxury tax. That is, a five-dollar pin will cost you $15. So you can see that they are really hit hard.

I suppose you are wondering what kind of a trip we had over here. Well, folks, I am not allowed to say too much because I might slip and the censor will cut out part of the letter, so I'll give you a few of the details.

For the most part, it was quite a long trip for my first ocean voyage, but we had a pretty good time of it. One thing that was hard to get used to at first was that they only had two meals a day, with coffee at noon. But they had a PX system aboard that allowed us to buy candy so it sort of filled in the gap.

Most of our time we spent reading to wile the time away, which got to be pretty long. There were also movies at nights, church services every evening, a jazz session now and then, and also a short program put on by the members on board, which was really good. Then every day we had boat drill, which sort of helped to break the monotony. Only bad thing about it was that for the first half of the trip I caught KP. By this time, I'm getting pretty good at it. In fact, the first sergeant thinks so much of me that he put me on it the first day we arrived in England, and I have had it again since then. But all in all, it was quite an experience.

Since we have been here, I have been kept pretty busy around here. What with details, hikes and lectures, I don't have a lot of time to myself.

Over here my mail has been coming through pretty regular, about six from Helen, three from you, one from Earle and another from Jimmy, plus a few that we don't talk about. I also received the money order that you sent, Mom, and thanks a lot.

But it looks like I won't have to use it after all. The main reason is that there is no place to spend it. By that I mean that they have no restaurants open and the beer isn't worthwhile buying. It costs about two shillings for two pints, approximately forty cents in our money. Even at that, it's no good and tastes like flat beer. And whisky is unheard of.

Last Tuesday evening I had a pass and went into town with Roberts. And believe me, it's the first time in ages that I ended up in a show [movie theater] on a pass. It's terrible. We had a couple ales and bitters, and couldn't [stand] it, so we finally ended up seeing Alice Faye in "The Girls We Left Behind." Most of the movies over here are American, and they are some of the latest. One strange thing about them is that it costs more to sit in the balcony than on the bottom floor, which they call stalls. Also, you may smoke in them.

As for buying supplies, we get ours through a PX system of our own. But even that is rationed. We are allowed only seven packs of cigarettes a week, which cost us five cents a pack, two razorblades a week, one bar of soap every two weeks, three candy bars a week with one package of gum. And the tops is one package of matches a week. How we are supposed to [make do with] that, I don't know.

So there are a few things I'd like to ask for. One is a cigarette lighter, if possible. I have one but it only works when it feels like, and that's damn seldom. If you find one, it will probably be in a hock shop. Also soap and candy.

In your last letter, you were talking about the cottage. I sure would give anything to be out there. I'll bet it's really nice since you started to repair it. But it probably won't be too long before we will be able to enjoy it like we used to.

Well, folks, I have to write a few letters yet, so I'll have to cut this short for now, so till then take care of yourselves and write soon and often.

Love to all,

Don

August 7, 1944: Around one o'clock, Roberts and myself borrowed a couple bicycles and rode all around the countryside for about four hours. It was really a lot of fun riding a bicycle again and getting a look at the country down the side roads.

As I told you in some of my last letters, England is still very old-fashioned in many ways, but I never quite imagined that I'd see some of the sights I saw. For instance, we saw these old-fashioned homes with straw or thatched roofs, old barns made of flagstones and looking older than the ages, people riding around in horse and buggies, other farmers driving their wagons loaded with goods, men cutting wheat with a sickle, roads so small that to pass a car you have to ride the sidewalks, and most of the homes in the crowded parts of the town built right on the streets…

In the evening, Roberts and I went to a different part of town than the one we usually go into. It's quite aways from camp, so the Army furnished transportation, and, as the old saying goes, "A good time was had by all."

Aside from being a little larger than the ones we are accustomed to over here it was still definitely English. The bobbies (cops) still wear white gloves and screwy head gear, lots of small pubs, soldiers and sailors, plenty of women, but they didn't interest me too much, and last but not least they still drive on the lefthand side of the street. Which by the way, damn near screwed me up good this morning. It happened this way:

I had to take a jeep out of the motor park and then take it uptown. Since I don't drive it much over here, out of habit I started up the right side of the street. Well, coming down the street on the same side was a darn truck and he wouldn't get out of the way. I figured I was in the right and made up my mind that if anyone moved it was going to be him. I guess he thought the same way, because he kept coming. I guess we might have met if one of the guys riding with me hadn't hollered. But that's one lesson I won't forget.

August 13, 1944: Last night, Toady and I went on pass for the first time in a week, and for a change, we really had a good time. Mostly drinking bitters and teaching some English dishes a little of our slang, and vice-versa. But that's as far as it went. We've already tried out the English dances, but to me and the rest of the

Hanging out with the guys somewhere in England. My dad, at left, has his hand on the shoulder of his buddy, Toady Roberts.

guys it looks as if these babes had ants in their pants. Mostly the two-step, and another one where everyone jumps around.

As for the music, it's okay if they have records, but if it's an orchestra, it's murder. I don't know why but the tempo is different and messes a guy all up. Even if it's all U.S. music, it can never compare with the States.

VICTORY WAITS
ON YOUR FINGERS—
KEEP 'EM FLYING, MISS U.S.A.
UNCLE SAM NEEDS STENOGRAPHERS! ★ GET CIVIL SERVICE INFORMATION AT YOUR LOCAL POST OFFICE
U.S. CIVIL SERVICE COMMISSION, WASHINGTON, D.C.

Chapter 16
France: A Most Interesting Place

Most of his letters from France have a dateline that reads, "somewhere in France," as the censors don't let him list more than four towns per letter. He writes of towns like Troyes, Commercy and Sens. Much of his time was spent in Normandy, where he reports the weather was rainy and cold.

According to a log he kept, titled "Travels of the 14th Battalion," he landed on Utah Beach on August 18, 1944, about two months after the D-Day landing, so things were pretty quiet. He was in France for most of the remainder of the year, staying primarily in abandoned homes, before departing for Luxembourg.

There seems to be a gap in his letter writing from December 10, 1944 through January 1, 1945. I'm guessing that may be because he was in the Battle of the Bulge, which raged from December 16, 1944 through January 25, 1945. In a letter dated in early January, he writes, "Don't say it! I know that I'm later than hell in dropping you a line, and I'm really sorry that it happened that way… But since my last letter, we have been kept pretty busy, and if you remember the headlines, you will understand why.

August 19, 1944: I suppose now is as good a time as any to tell you that I don't have any more worries of England on my mind. No more bitters or ale, or bobbies, left-handed drivers or any more of that Limey slang. To make matters short, it all boils down to the fact that we are now in France.

Just because I am in France, please don't worry any more than you do about me. I am safe and feeling swell. We are now eating rations and they taste pretty good for a change. But I suppose that in time they will get pretty tiresome.

What I have seen of France so far doesn't give me much to talk about. Mostly dust, dirty farms, cows and chickens. There are a few kids around here but they look pretty rough. Which isn't so hard to understand when one thinks what kind of hell they have been put through in the last four years.

Changing the subject, I suppose you are wondering what kind of trip we had across the channel. Well, it was pretty nice. Good sleeping accommodations and swell chow. In fact, the Navy put out the best food I've eaten since my Army career started. By the way, did you know that I have been in the Army 18 months today? One year and a half. A long time.

August 22, 1944: So far, aside from loss of sleep and lack of home cooking, I've got no kick [slang for complaint] coming. Since our arrival here in France, we have seen plenty of country, people and also the so-called "price of war."

Honestly, moms, the people back home have no idea of what war is at all. For some of those chronic gripers, they should be brought over here and made to live here awhile.

The people over here have been living under German rule for the last four years, and now that they are free again, they are just about nuts with joy. When our convoys pass on the roads through towns, people just drop everything and line the roads and streets to see us pass, and believe me, that's when one sees how they feel about us over here. Everyone waves, throws kisses, flowers, apples, tomatoes and all kinds of fruit. But the best part is the wine they pass around.

Over here I've seen sights that I had read about but never quite believed.
For instance, I saw real milkmaids carrying two buckets of milk suspended
by a yoke around their neck. The first thing I thought about when I saw
them was how would Dot and Smitty fit in here? But after a moment's
hesitation, I knew it would be no dice.

- August 29, 1944, France

August 29, 1944: Well, people, in the last three of four months, I have seen quite a bit of this old world, but of it all, I believe France is the most interesting.

Most of the farm people over here wear those big wooden shoes with felt liners in them. When they go indoors, they just slip them off and leave them on the doorstep…

Another sight I had heard of but never quite believed was the use of toilets on street corners. When a person walks into one you can see from the chest up and the knees down, and believe me, it doesn't require a great deal of imagination to know what is going on.

For the most part, the people travel by bicycle or horse and buggy. And in some cases, they are driving automobiles that were captured from the Germans. Also, we occasionally see some of those charcoal burners that are used instead of gasoline.

Over here in our traveling around we have seen plenty of the so-called ravages of war: cities blown apart, fires, automobiles and German wreckage lining the road, bridges blown out and all the rest. After seeing a little of this, one can be plenty thankful that the States were spared this plight.

But of it all, I believe the most remarkable thing over here is the people. After four years of occupation, and then to be free. One has no idea of the joy the people go through. And believe me, they think the Yanks are tops.

When convoys go through towns, people first line the streets, windows and doorways. And if you happen to slow down, they run out with flowers, apples, cherries, tomatoes, bread, wine, cider and even cognac. Besides that, it seems as if a guy is running for mayor after shaking hands with them. It really does something to a guy when people are that grateful. It sure beats England all to hell.

I guess the hardest part of getting along over here is to understand their language. By this time, I'm getting a little more used to it and can understand a little of it. Right now I'm learning how to pronounce a few greetings and the names of food. The one we find most useful is "des cigarettes por du vin." To you it means cigarettes for wine, and believe me it comes in mighty handy.

French Towns: Sights and Smells

He writes about his impressions of French country towns in a letter dated September 16, 1944.

Another thing that might interest you are the towns around here. The large cities are quite modern and look a little like some of the towns back home. But these country towns, they're terrible.

Honestly, I've never seen anything like it before. Most of the homes are right on the street, with the barn attached to the house. It's nothing to see people standing in their doorways and having the horses and cattle dropping their load right in front of the door.

Another thing they do is to pile the manure right in front of the house and leave it there until it rots. God, what an odor, and the people don't seem to mind it a bit.

But even at that, I guess I'm not one to judge how the people live. Even if most of these people don't live in the most sanitary conditions, it still doesn't take anything away from them as a swell bunch of people.

October 2, 1944: The best part over here is that we have taken over a small French town, and we are now living in houses. Of course, most of them are bare, but it's a place to sleep out of the rain and cold…

Well, folks, we've finally got it made. The reason is we are now living in a house. Our whole party of 19 men have two big rooms to themselves. The rooms are fairly clean and have tables, mirrors and stoves. For lighting, we have two gas lanterns in our room and a couple headlights working off a truck battery.

- October 5, 1944, France

October 11, 1944: You know now that we are living in houses and have it pretty nice, but that isn't enough for us. We've got to have the best, so we are kept busy improving it.

Since we have been here, we have put in a stove (about 24-by-15) in our room, which accommodates 10 men. I'll admit it sounds crowded but we get along pretty good. Getting back to the stove, it will heat three one-gallon cans of water at a time and also has an oven. The best part is that it throws plenty of heat, and in turn solves the problem of wet clothes.

Another thing we have added is lights. Since there is no electricity here, it looks as if we had to depend on candles. But here is where American ingenuity came in. We got together some old or extra headlights, some drop cord and a car battery. Now we've got all the light one could want.

But I believe the best added feature is our beds we made yesterday. Before we were sleeping on the floor with a little straw under us. Now we have five double-deckers, share a top one and they are really swell.

October 15, 1944: I know I told you a little bit about this town we're living in but I'll give you a bit more detail. For the most part it's just an ordinary French village, with a church, store and one tavern. The main street is paved, but the sidewalks are scarce. The people around here use all kinds of transportation.

It's nothing to see a cart going down the street drawn by a couple horses and an ox. Other means are wheel barrels, a few German trucks, and some of their own trucks run by charcoal burners. A few of the luckier ones are getting gas to run their cars. Where they get it is beyond me. Others use bikes.

In this town, most of the people have a few cattle, chickens and geese, and they are always roaming the streets. As for the way the people live and dress, they do pretty good considering what they've got. In almost all cases, all the French homes I've been in have been darn clean, even those that have the barn attached to the houses.

> *One wonders how they can ever keep their places clean with all the mud, manure and dirt around their places. But they've got a sure solution. For working, the people wear wooden shoes with felt fillers. So when they are about to go in they just kick off the shoes and walk around in their slippers.*
>
> *- October 15, 1944, France*

Then on Sundays and holidays, they really celebrate and dress up in their fanciest duds, including leather shoes.

Getting back to the dirt and people, one wonders at first how anyone could live in it. But after seeing a few examples of the youngsters about 85, one comes to the opinion that you just can't kill them. The kids are always full of pep, rosy cheeks, friendly and aggravating as all heck. Right now, I'm beating off the kid next door. Someone started to teach him to count in English, but he has

Yes, They Still Have Town Criers

Following is an excerpt from a letter from France, dated December 9, 1944.

Say, moms, something just happened here that is really strange. The town crier just went through hollering the news out.

They don't have radios around here so they elect some old guy to walk through the streets shouting out the news. But to do it properly is really an art.

To understand it, you just have to get the picture:

Here he comes down the street, an old ragged man with long dirty gray moustache, stained slightly with tobacco. Around his shoulders, he's got an old drum that looks as if it was through the last war. He comes up the street, stops, looks around, takes out his sticks and beats the hell out of the drum.

After his audience is big enough, he slowly puts the sticks back in their case, spits the tobacco in his hand and then starts yelling his head off. Boy, you never saw anyone that swaggers as much, or thinks more of himself, than the town crier.

only got to 29 so far. Right now he's whispering in my ear, 28-29, 28-29, thinking that I'll tell him the next one.

October 28, 1944: We're still living in houses and are continuing improvements all the time. Now we have added a few mirrors, easy chairs, and tables and lanterns, all of which we found in wrecked cars or homes.

As for the atmosphere of these towns, they smell just like the old country. It seems as if it's a must in these country towns to have a pile of manure piled right in front of the front door. The manure is bad enough, but they usually leave it lay around till it's rotten. Boy, some of these towns have a smell that you will never forget. In a way, it's all its own, and I'm satisfied to leave it that way.

Neufchâtel-en-Bray
Aumale
Poix
AMIENS
235
Ham
Forges-les-Eaux
Grandvilliers
Montdidier
Roye
Noyon
Breteuil
Cuvilly
ROUEN
Marseille-le-P.
Beauvais
St. Just en-Ch.
Compiègne
Gournay
Boos
Clermont
Creil
38 Soissons
Les Andelys
Gisors
158
134
Les Thilliers-en-Vexin
Chantilly
Senlis
Villers-Cotterêts
Pacy-s.-Eure
Vernon
125
Beaumont
Château Thier
Mantes s.-S.
Bonnières
Pontoise
Épône
64 Meaux
La Fer s.-Jou
St. Germain
Couilly
Coulommie
Houdan
Versailles
PARIS
La Ferté-Gaucher
Dreux
Rambouillet
Brie C.-R.
Fontenay
Guignes-s.-R.
Provins
Châteauneuf-en-Th.
Maintenon
Corbeil
Melun
Montereau f.-Yonne
Chartres
Ablis
Authon-la-P.
Étampes
Fontainebleau
67
120
116
Angerville
Allaines
Bonneval
Janville
Malesherbes
Pithiviers
Sens
Artenay
Courtenay
231
Orléans
Montargis
Joigny
Beaugency
Châteauneuf-s.-L.
172
Blois
La Motte
Auxerre
114
174

Chapter 17
French Women: Ooh La La

August 29, 1944: Another strange thing is that most of these people seem to be well-dressed, and they do have a little makeup. They tell us that everyone is wearing their best in celebration. Another thing is that these women for the most part really know how to dress and fix themselves up. I know because we've seen many of them and they're plenty sharp. It just brings out the old wolf in me.

September 8, 1944: Another thing that I like about France is they have many good-looking women. Besides being nice looking, they really are neat in appearance, keep their hair fixed up and know how to wear makeup. In other words, they sure beat the hell out of these English women that I have seen.

The Most Beautiful Women in France

*On October 7, 1944, he writes about encountering
the three most beautiful women in France.*

Say, folks, you ought to see the difficulty that I'm writing under now.

I'm sitting at a table with a gas lantern for light with three of the most beautiful women in France looking over my shoulder trying to read what I'm writing. The only trouble is they can't be over 10 at the most. So what's a guy going to do?

Right now they are giggling to beat hell. The reason why is that I tried to pronounce their names. Boy, some of them sure are tongue twisters.

October 2, 1944: In the house [where we are living] where we have the kitchen located, there is an old French woman living there, and boy the guys really get a kick out of her. She must be close to 65 and is nice and friendly. In fact, I believe she has taken over from the cooks. The reason I say that is at every meal she is out there watching the guys eat, and that's when she really comes into her own. If she sees the cooks or the guys waste too much, she really raises hell with them in French. Of course, we can't understand her, but her expressions and actions are all that are needed to understand what she means. By the way, she'll be in her glory tonight because we are having steak, and from the looks of her when they were frying them, it will be anyone's tail if they throw any of it out. God only knows who would do such a thing.

December 2, 1944: I don't believe I answered your question about how these French people dress. Well, moms, in the city they look much the same as the American girls, although I have to admit that some of the hats they wear are all French. Boy, some of them are really a laugh.

As for me falling for any of these women over here, that's the farthest thing from my mind. All I want to do is get the hell out of here, and back home again. Anyway, I'll take the American Girl any day to either the French or English.

Chapter 18
Luxembourg, Belgium and Holland: Meeting Locals

My dad was in Luxembourg from late 1944 through early 1945, later moving through Belgium and Holland before arriving in Germany in February of 1945.

January 29, 1945, Luxembourg: As I said before, there are some nice people, and there are some that are a pain in the neck. For instance, take the last place we were in.

It was a pretty good place. It had running water, electric lights, radio and a good stove. But there were two guys living there that were about sixty years old and harder to get along with than Sister Aloyse [a teacher at St. Rita High School in Detroit]. And you know how she was.

They'd worry about how we treated the room, if we'd taken our overshoes off before coming in, if we'd touch their

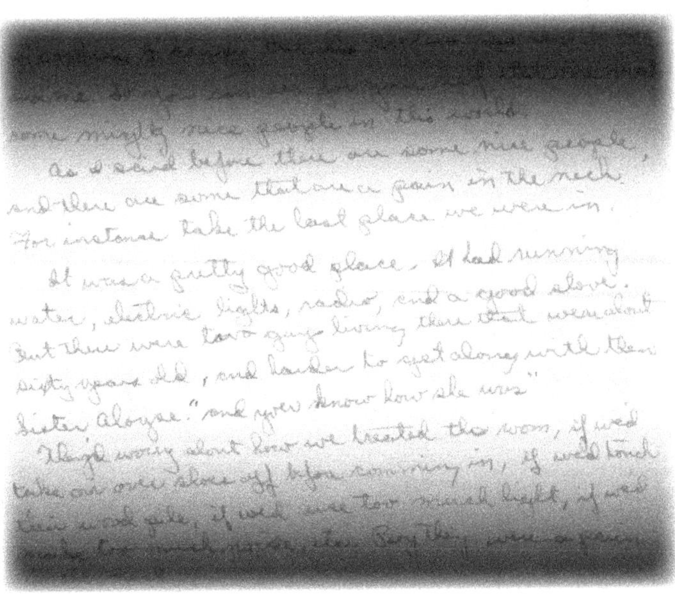

woodpile, if we'd use too much light, if we'd make too much noise, etc. Boy, they were a pain in the neck.

It turned out that they were married and had evacuated their wives. Well, one day, the old lady shows up, the other weasel took off, and everything was OK. Before we left there, butter was just dripping out of his month. Nothing was too good for us. He gave us fresh eggs, milk, apples, pears and anything we wanted.

Before his wife came, you just about had to twist his arm to get a drink of water. It was just a case of where he wanted everything and didn't want to give anything in return.

I suppose it just narrows down to that old saying about women and proves to be true once more: You can't get along with them, and you can't get along without them."

A couple of swell people and a little imp if there ever was one. The people gave us their beds and most of their rations, Verviers, Belgium, June 1945.

Some of the kids who hung around us. Quite a few of them speak English.

These kids pestered the hell out of us for C-rations. They claimed they wanted them for souvenirs: "a new angle," February 1945.

Help Him
Every $3.00 you put into War Bonds buys 144 rifle bullets
Help Yourself
Every $3.00 you put into War Bonds brings you back $4.00
FOR VICTORY
AT LEAST 10% OF YOUR PAY EVERY PAYDAY

Chapter 19
Germany in 1945: Pretty Scenery, Bombed-out Towns, Friendly People

In a letter to my mother, dated March 9, 1945, he writes about what Germany looks like after the bombings, and how the German people behave toward American troops. He seems to struggle to understand why, after all the atrocities committed by Hitler and his Army, the German people are so friendly to them.

March 4, 1945, Germany: There is no getting around it that the Old Country has some pretty scenery. But believe me when I say that the U.S. can duplicate everything they have and yet go them one better.

One thing I can't get used to is the houses they have over here. All of them I have seen have been made of stone, brick or clay, and look as if they have been standing for centuries and are plenty tired of life, especially these houses in the country. I don't believe these people ever heard of sanitation or else they just don't give a damn.

March 9, 1945: It's ten o'clock now, and I've just heard the news headlines. To us guys, it sounds darn good, and it looks as if we are really riding the hell out of the Krauts. At the rate we're going now, something is bound to pop.

I suppose you noticed the heading on my letter, "Germany at last." And believe me, it sure looks good to see these Germans suffering for a change. They caused a lot of hell for the world in their short reign, and I'm only afraid that they will not get repaid in full for it.

Of what I have seen of Germany, I can't say much for what's left. It's only lately that we have been able to find a house here that has a decent roof left or a window in it. For the most part, they consist

German Women: That's Another Story

In letters from March, 1945, he writes about the women he encounters.

As for the women, well, that's another story. I suppose you've all heard about the non-fraternizing order. It's a 65-cent fine, or worse, if you're caught fooling around with any Germans.

The women are pretty sharp looking, and to guys who have been overseas anywhere from a year to four, they even look better. Some of them are more than friendly, and that makes it twice as rough. But as far as I'm concerned, they can have them. I don't want anything to do with them…

When the civilians are let out, they look like just about any other crowd in the States, although it looks as if they breed their farm women like their horses, big and strong. Some of these women look as if they could pull a plow all day long without any great difficulty.

Don't get me wrong, they are not all like that because there are many that would do justice to a bathing suit.

mainly of a basement filled with trash. In other words, the towns just don't exist anymore.

As for the people, I don't think much of them. Anyone who would fall for the line that Hitler passed out and commit such atrocities sure don't rate with me. On most of the walls left standing, there are messages painted such as "We love Hitler," "We will never surrender," etc.

Yet these people have the gall to come out and act friendly. Stand around and smile and call us "comrade." Comrade, hell. I wouldn't trust one of them across the street from me.

The people on the whole look fairly well fed and clothed. In fact, they look much like the people do in the States. As for their living quarters, most of them live in bomb shelters because there are no more homes. And those that are left, well, we take over.

March 12, 1945: The place we're staying in is really swell. In fact, it's the best we've had since leaving the States. Big rooms with beds, stoves, tables, dressers, curtains, polished floors, etc. In fact, everything a guy could want. Even holy pictures on the wall.

The people seem to be well fed and are dressed darn well. Most of the families own either a car, motorcycle or a couple bikes. So it looks as if they did pretty well for themselves at one time or another…

As for the looks of the country, I'd say at one time it was sure great farming land. It's pretty level and seems to get enough rain. Only now it looks pretty lifeless. I guess it's been farmed pretty heavily for the last few years.

One good thing they have over here is highways. They are the best I've seen in Europe and make me think of the States. Occasionally we see gas pumps and restaurants. Believe me, it sure brings back memories.

April 4, 1945: Well, moms, they have finally allowed us to tell you a few of the towns we have been around since we hit Germany. Three of them that won't be too hard to locate are Aachen, Julich and Monchengladbach.

Roberts and I were just talking about one of the places we stayed in. Boy, we really enjoyed ourselves while we could.

It was just a farmhouse and barns that were all knocked to hell. About all that was left that was any good was the barn where they kept the livestock.

The civilians had left so when we finished work at night we would water and feed the horses, cows, pigs, chickens, calves and anything else that could walk. We even milked the cows and fed the milk to the young calves that they had put in a pen. By the way, I'm an accomplished milker now.

But the most fun was the horses they have. While we were there, we figured they needed a little exercise, so we just put the bridles on and took off. Honestly, it was more darn fun than I've had in a coon's age, but for a week after I was plenty stiff. And confidentially I believe I sprung another inch or so between my legs.

On the last one, it was another big farm, but this one was in good condition and the owner was still there with his family. While at that place we didn't do too much riding of horses. But they did have a motorcycle and a car. And believe me, we really gave them quite a workout.

The car was German made, two-cylinder job and burned a mixture of benzol and diesel oil. It smoked plenty but would do about 40. As for the motorcycle, it was also German and seeing as it was the first time I rode one, I had quite a time.

June 10, 1945: Well, honey, I believe the most news I have is that we have moved again. This time it's down to the 7th Army in a large city named Backnang. In case you'd like to look it up on a map, we are located 20 miles northeast of Stuttgart, which is about 125 miles south of Frankfurt. So you can see that our move was quite long. Approximately 350 miles, and took us better than a day and a half to make it.

Believe me kid, 350 miles of riding in a GI vehicle isn't much fun, but we had a fairly good time. We saw lots of the country and people, which was interesting.

Glimpses of Army Life in Germany

Larry and me in Krefeld, Germany, February 1945.

Moving from Juchen to Kamp-Lintfort, and awaiting the crossing of the Rhine, Germany, March 1945.

Small, Davies and me at the swimming pool, Backnang, Germany, June 1945.

Niemi, me and Roberts with schnapps and beer, June 1945.

Me, Niemi and Marsh at the airport, June 1945.

Leaving dear old Backnang, July 1945.

Part of the old gang before we left for the States, Backnang, July 1945.

Travels of the 14th. Observation Battalion
(Landed on Utah Beach August 1?, 1944)

1. Ste. Mere Eglise (
2. Caretan
3. Countances
4. Granville
5. Avranches
6. Fougeres
7. Laval
8. Le Mans
9. Orleans------------Loire River
10. Montargis---------Loing River
11. Sens--------------Yonne River
12. Troyes------------Seine River
13. Chalons sur-------Marne River
14. Revigny
15. Bar Le Duc
16. Commercy----------Euese River
17. St. Mihiel
18. Gironville (Fort)
19. Thiacourt
20. Pont a Mousson
21. Toul--------------Rhin River
22. St. Nicholas
23. Vezuglese
24. Bayon------------Moselle River
25. Rosiers   (Sept.16)
26. Luneville
27. Remerville   (Sept.18)
28. Nancy
29. Pompey
30. Champenoux   (Sept.25)
31. Custines
32. Gremercy
33. Leyer   (Oct. 25)
34. Ajoncourt((Nov. 10)
35. Delme   (Nov. 12)
36. Chateau Salines
37. Lucy   (Nov. 14)
38. Morhange   (Nov. 19)
39. Erstroff   (Nov. 22)
40. Gros Tenquin   (Nov. 23)
        "THANKSGIVING DAY"
41. Heller
42. Leywiller   (Nov. 28)
43. St. Jean
44. Puttelange
45. Hundling   (Dec. 6)
        "MY FOUR DAY PASS"
46. Siltzhieme   (Dec. 15)
47. Bliesbrucken   (Dec. 16)
48. St. Avold
49. Metz
50. Dieden Hoffen

LUXEMBURG

51. Hunsdorf
52. Luxemburg City
53. Lorensweiller
54. Junglister   (Dec. 22)
        "CHRISTMAS DAY"
55. Mersch
56. Schrondweiller   (Dec. 28)
        "NEW YEARS DAY"
        "MY BIRTHDAY"
57. Fells
58. Medernach
59. Ettelbruck-------Sure River
60. Diekirch
61. Stegen   (Jan. 2?)
62. Schlern
63. Niierfeulen   (Jan. 24)
64. Wiltz

BELGIUM

65. Vaux
66. Bastonge
67. Troviergas-------Our River
68. St. Vith
69. Dinant
70. Namur
71. Tongres
72. Libin

HOLLAND

73. Maastritch
74. Herrelen
75. Kirkrade
76. Falkenburg

GERMANY

77. Aachen   (Feb. 6)
78. Forelmunster
79. Wurslen
80. Alsdorf   (Feb. 7)
81. Julich-----------Roer River
82. Serest   (Feb. 28)
83. Rodingen   (Mar. 2)
84. Juchen   (Mar. 4)
85. Rhedyt
86. Munchen Gladbeck
87. Osterath   (Mar. 6)
88. Neuss
89. Nuls

GERMANY CONTD-

90. Krefield
91. Kamp Lintfort   (Mar. 11)
92. Rhineburg
93. Buderich
94. Wesel
95. Dusseldorf
96. Spellen-----------Rhine River "TUCKERS RADICAL TERRORS"
97. Vorde   (Mar. 28)
98. Kirchellen   (Mar. 30)
        "MET A, PLAGENS"
99. Polsum   (Apr. 1)
100. Krey   (12, Apr)
101. Gladbeck   (Apr. 3)
102. Gelsenkirchen
103. Essen
104. Remkersleben   (Apr. 16)
105. Meitzendorf   (Apr. 17)
106. Ebendorf   (Apr. 20)
        "V.E.DAY-MAY 8, 1945"
107. Magdeburg--------Elbe River
108. Recklinghausen
109. Datteln
110. Bochum
111. Bielfield
112. Lemgo
113. Barntrop
114. Hamlen
115. Else
116. Helmstedt
117. Wittigen
118. Dedelsdorf   (May 10)
        "AIR FIELD"
119. Brunswick
120. Hannover
121. Peine
122. Dortmund
123. Celle
124. Northeim   This trip was
125. Bisleben   346 miles, from
126. Gottingen   Dedelsdorf to
127. Eisnach   Backnang.
128. Meiningen
129. Wzrzburg
130. Neustadt
131. Bad Mergentheim
132. Crailsheim
133.Schwab Hall
134. Backnang   (June 3)
God only knows where we'll be next.

"FINIS"

—CHINA BOUND—

Signed –
        T.D.Berry

NOTE

The cities with dates after them, are those that I have lived in. Also the paticular inncident that happened there, is located directly beneath the town.

This list does not include all the cities I've been in. But only the more important ones.

The trip from Krey No.100, to Remkersleben, No.104, was 284 miles.

The trip from Ebendorf No.106, to Dedelsdorf No.118, was 64 miles.

104

Chapter 20
The End of the Journey

The letters from my dad end abruptly with a letter from Camp Chaffee, Arkansas, dated September 24, 1945. The war had come to an end in early September after the Japanese surrendered.
He returned from overseas after more than two years. It's unclear from one of his letters whether he is preparing to be discharged or whether he might become part of the "Army of occupation," perhaps in Germany, where his younger brother, Earl, served after the war ended.

The only time he wrote about his future plans, or lack thereof, was in a letter dated May 2, 1945, when he learned that Hitler had died, six days before the war ended in Europe and four months before the Japanese surrender.

"With the news as it is," he wrote, "a guy can't help but wonder what is going to happen to us when the war in Europe is finally over. In fact, it's the main topic of conversation around here. Everyone is figuring out his chances of getting out. As for myself, I'm not planning on a darn thing. The way I figure it, I've got too little time in, too little time overseas, not old enough and no dependents. So just taking a quick glance at my record, I can't help but feel that 'they've got me where they want me.'

"Some of the guys figure we're due for the C.B.I. [China, Burma India Theater], while others think we are a sure thing for the Army of occupation. Others think we'll go back to the States. As for myself, I just don't think, only hope."

When my dad returned from the war, I remember him saying that he had a hard time finding a job. His father, who had been a carpenter and supervisor on construction sites throughout the U.S., suggested he get a job as an electrician. He felt that it was a "clean" job, one where you didn't get your hands dirty and could wear a white shirt and tie.

My dad subsequently went to a job interview for an electrician's apprentice and was told he couldn't get a job if he didn't have a father or other family member in the electrician's union. Evidently nepotism was rampant in the industry. After having served his country for more than two years, my dad got extremely angry about the unfairness of it all — and prepared to bolt out of the room.

"Wait a minute," the interviewer said. "I heard that the president of Turner Electric Company in Detroit is looking for a truck driver. Why don't you go there?" My dad did, enjoying his time as a truck driver and eventually having a successful career as a salesman in the electrical industry, serving as a vice president of sales at one point. Throughout his career, he considered just about everyone — customers and colleagues alike — to be a friend. In fact, one of his favorite ways of addressing people was "Friend."

My dad's optimistic world view and cheerful outlook undoubtedly were key to why he survived and even thrived during his time in the Army. He enjoyed the guys in his battalion and the people he met along the way.

An excerpt from one letter, where he writes about the time he spent a weekend with the family of one of his Army buddies when he was stationed in Washington state, stands out to me: "The best part was that Mrs. Roberts, his mother, made my favorite pie for me. Lemon for me and apple for her son. Besides that, she gave up her bed for me to sleep in. A big innerspring mattress with crisp, cool sheets. You can talk about your nice people but I doubt if you can beat them."

My dad seemed to genuinely love people and they generally responded in kind. I always thought he would have made a great priest as he seemed to love the people in his sphere equally, as opposed to just being committed to his nuclear family. He would get just as excited about a nephew's accomplishments as one of my own. I was never jealous as, being an only child, I got plenty of attention!

In looking at his behavior from today's perspective, in which people are much more well-versed in psychological issues, it seems that people who have positive expectations tend to attract positive things to them, while those with a negative outlook often attract negative experiences. It certainly seemed to work that way for my dad.

I'm also reminded of a quote from Abraham Lincoln: "A man's about as happy as he makes up his mind to be." Since Lincoln suffered from depression, his words carry a certain weight. It's interesting to consider that one's decision making can play a key role in how happy or unhappy a person is.

While many servicemen married their sweethearts as soon as they returned from the war in 1945 — sparking the Baby Boom — my parents didn't marry until 1948, three years after his return. My mom said that in addition to dates with her, he spent a lot of time hanging out with buddies at one bar or another. "There was a lot of drinking going on in those days after the end of the war," she recalled.

My mom sometimes lamented that his letters to her weren't very romantic — that he mostly wrote about his experiences. But I did find some exceptions, which I included in the "Romance" chapter.

My mom was a bookkeeper at National Bank of Detroit in downtown Detroit before their marriage — and for three months afterward. She told me that married women at the bank were required to leave their job three months after marriage during that time period to open up jobs to the returning "heroes." It was all part of the social mores of time.

Looking at it from today's perspective, it certainly seems unfair. I remember my mom telling me she suffered from depression for a long period of time after leaving her job.

In the early years of their marriage, their lives were filled with plenty of parties with family and friends, as well as vacations in northern Michigan. My dad was an avid amateur photographer, so his experiences were well-documented.

I was born in 1955, when my mom was 30 and my dad was 31.

His post-war life was productive, well-rounded and generally happy. He lived to the age of 79 — quite an achievement for someone who had a family history of heart disease. His mother died at 59, his brother Earl at the same age as his mom, and his second-to-youngest brother, Wally, at 55. My mom outlived my dad by 12 years.

I found his letters from the war entertaining and often instructive, which is why I wanted to share them with others. They reinforced the fun-loving, energetic, people-loving person I came to know and love.

I regret not asking him more details about his war experience, especially about the Battle of the Bulge, a key battle of World War II. I'm sure he would have told me all about it if I would have asked. I know that many men from that era avoided talking about their wartime experiences because they were so traumatic.

The only time I recall him getting emotional about his war experience was when he told a story about driving by an outhouse that had been blown up. A German soldier, who was dead, was still sitting on the toilet. That story brought tears to his eyes. Perhaps it was because in that everyday moment, he could see that we all share a common humanity.

I hope that through this book I've been able to offer some stories and insights that might benefit others in some way — or at least give readers a few chuckles. I know that writing it has given my life another layer of meaning, and I'm thankful to have had the opportunity to share my dad's stories.

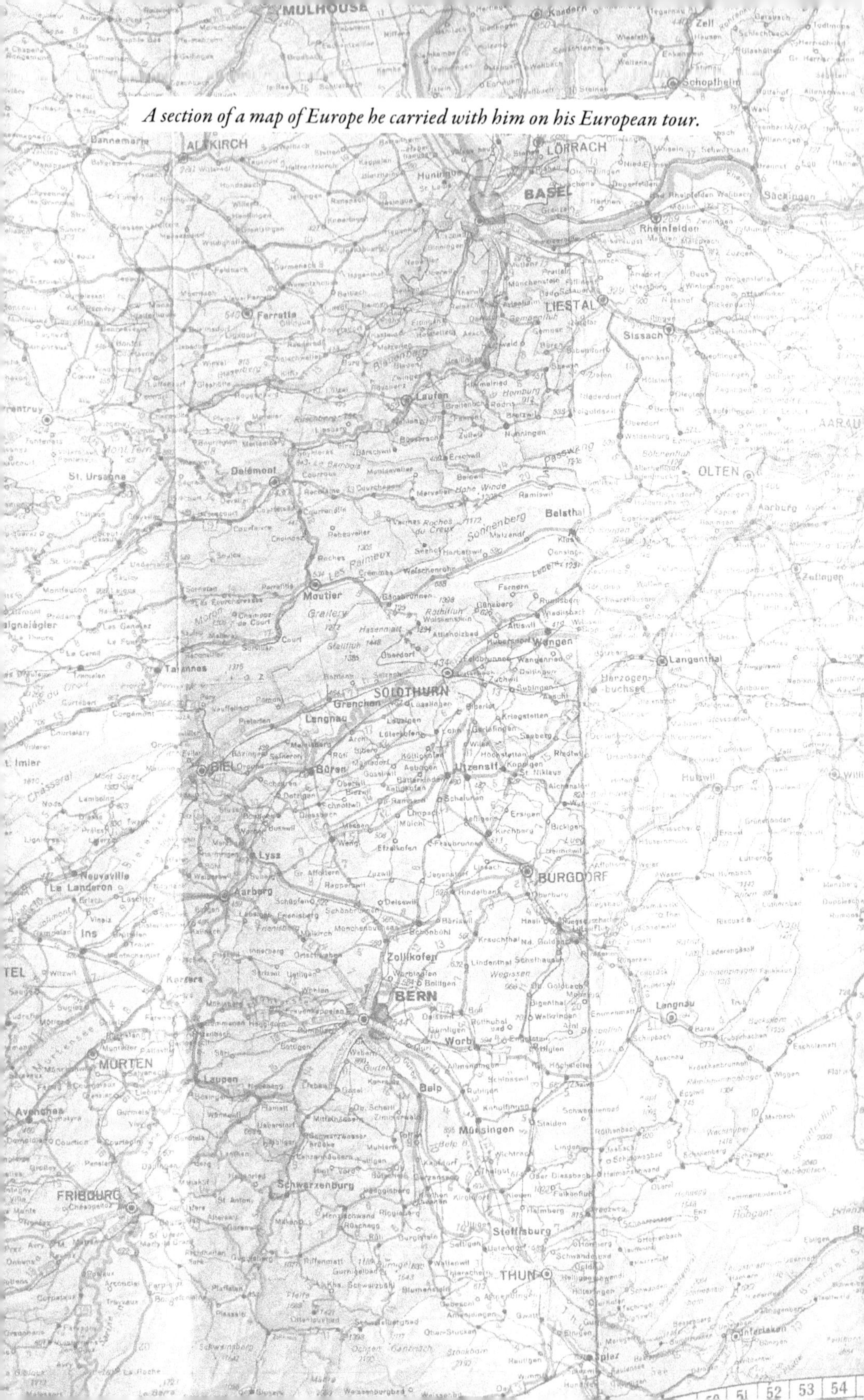

A section of a map of Europe he carried with him on his European tour.

www.ingramcontent.com/pod-product-compliance
Lightning Source LLC
Chambersburg PA
CBHW041335120726
48005CB00014B/2271